T0093274

Fëdor Khitruk

This book is a first and long-awaited study of the directorial work of the animation master Fëdor Khitruk (1917–2012), an artist who formed in the tradition of classical cel animation only to break the conventions once he turned into a director; a liaison between artists and authorities; a personality who promoted daring films to be created in the Soviet Union dominated by socialist realism; and a teacher and supporter of young artists that continued to carry on his legacy long after the Soviet empire collapsed.

Fëdor Khitruk: A Look at Soviet Animation through the Work of One Master reveals Khitruk's mastery in the art of the moving image and his critical role as a director of films that changed the look of Soviet animation and its relation to the animation world within and beyond the Eastern Bloc. Based on archival research, personal interviews, published memoirs, and perceptive analyses of Khitruk's production of films for children and adults, this study is a must-read for scholars in Soviet art and culture as well as readers fascinated by traditional animation art.

Laura Pontieri, PhD taught Soviet cinema and European animation at the University of Toronto for many years, appeared as a speaker at academic conferences and cinema events, and published several articles and reviews on Russian and Czech animation in North American and European journals. She is the author of the book *Soviet Animation and the Thaw of the 1960s: Not Only for Children* (John Libbey Publishing, 2012).

Focus Animation

The Focus Animation Series aims to provide unique, accessible content that may not otherwise be published. We allow researchers, academics, and professionals the ability to quickly publish high impact, current literature in the field of animation for a global audience.

This series is a fine complement to the existing, robust animation titles available through CRC Press/Focal Press.

Series Editor Chris Robinson is the Artistic Director of the Ottawa International Animation Festival (OIAF) and is a well-known figure in the animated film world. We welcome any submissions to help grow the wonderful content we are striving to provide to the animation community.

Pamela Taylor Turner
Infinite Animation: The Life and Work of Adam Beckett

Marco Bellano
Václav Trojan Music Composition in Czech Animated Films

Adrijana Ruzic
Michael Dudok de Wit A Life in Animation

Giannalberto Bendazzi
A Moving Subject

Max Bannah
Wharfie Animator: Harry Reade, The Sydney Waterfront, and the Cuban Revolution

Chris Robinson
Mad Eyed Misfits: Writings on Indie Animation

Dennis Tupicoff
Life in Death: My Animated Films 1976–2020

Olga Bobrowska
Chinese Animated Film and Ideology, 1940s–1970s: Fighting Puppets

Liisa Vähäkylä
Nordic Animation Balancing the East and the West

https://www.routledge.com/Focus-Animation/book-series/CRCFOCUSANI

Photos courtesy of Fëdor Khitruk.

Fëdor Khitruk
A Look at Soviet Animation through the Work of One Master

Laura Pontieri

CRC Press
Taylor & Francis Group
Boca Raton London New York

CRC Press is an imprint of the
Taylor & Francis Group, an **Informa** business

First edition published 2024
by CRC Press
2385 Executive Center Drive, Suite 320, Boca Raton, FL 33431

and by CRC Press
4 Park Square, Milton Park, Abingdon, Oxon, OX14 4RN

CRC Press is an imprint of Taylor & Francis Group, LLC

© 2024 Laura Pontieri

Library of Congress Cataloging-in-Publication Data
Names: Pontieri, Laura, author.
Title: Fëdor Khitruk : a look at Soviet animation through the work of one master / Laura Pontieri.
Description: Boca Raton, FL : CRC Press, 2023. |
Includes bibliographical references and index.
Identifiers: LCCN 2023002725 (print) | LCCN 2023002726 (ebook) |
ISBN 9781032058795 (paperback) | ISBN 9781032022574 (hardback) |
ISBN 9781003199625 (ebook)
Subjects: LCSH: Khitruk, F. S.–Criticism and interpretation. |
Animated films–Russia (Federation)–History and criticism.
Classification: LCC NC1766.R92 K4937 2023 (print) | LCC NC1766.R92 (ebook) |
DDC 791.43/340947—dc23/eng/20230215
LC record available at https://lccn.loc.gov/2023002725
LC ebook record available at https://lccn.loc.gov/2023002726

ISBN: 978-1-032-02257-4 (hbk)
ISBN: 978-1-032-05879-5 (pbk)
ISBN: 978-1-003-19962-5 (ebk)

DOI: 10.1201/9781003199625

Typeset in Times
by codeMantra

To *Dan*

Contents

Acknowledgments

I would like to remember and acknowledge here my dear colleague Giannalberto Bendazzi, an extraordinarily dedicated and passionate scholar of animation. I miss a friend and point of reference for everything about animation for the past twenty years. I wish he were here to read this finished project, of which he was an enthusiastic supporter.

I owe my gratitude to many people who helped me gather information during these atypical two years (and the previous twenty), especially to Georgii Borodin, Sergei Kapkov, Natasha Berezovaia, Mikhail Tumelia, Sergei Seregin, and Mikhail Aldashin, who have been constantly ready to reply to my questions and to seek answers to my research challenges. I would like to thank Pavel Shvedov for his dedication to Russian animation and his assistance, and Aleksandr Gerasimov for his help with material. I would also like to express my gratitude to Fedya Khitruk for kindly sharing photos and information about his grandfather. I'm grateful to Soyuzmultfilm for the copyright license for all illustrations and Sean Connelly at CRC Press for believing in this project.

On a more personal note, many thanks to Alison Goddard, for her friendship and invaluable comments and suggestions. And thanks to Veronika Ambros for her constant encouragement and feedback. I'm beyond grateful to my girls for their patience and cheering, and to my husband for believing in me and supporting in many ways all my peculiar projects.

This book is an extension of preliminary studies on Soviet animation of the 1960s. While the discussion of Khitruk's first two directorial films, *Story of a Crime* and *Man in the Frame*, will not be completely novel for those acquainted with my previous work, I expand here my earlier analyses and offer a panoramic view of the entire production of Khitruk as a director, as much as the limitation of space allowed. Much of my research stems from printed and online material gathered throughout the years, as well as archival material consulted almost two decades ago, which gave me the opportunity to write this book even though traveling was out of question. I am still indebted to those people who helped me at that early time, and most of all to Fëdor Savel'evich Khitruk himself, who opened his house for me many years ago and whose work continues to fascinate me to this day.

NOTE ON TRANSLITERATION AND TRANSLATIONS

This book follows a simplified Library of Congress System for transliterating Russian. Only well-known names appear in the text in a standard anglicized spelling, namely Mayakovsky, Norstein, Eisenstein, Petrushevskaya, Yutkevich, Stanislavsky, Meyerhold, and the studio Soyuzmultfilm. Unless otherwise noted, all translations are my own.

Preface

Fëdor Savel'evich Khitruk (1917–2012) found himself in the animation world quite by chance. He liked to draw, he was talented and fast, and, after finishing art school,[1] he entertained the idea of working as an illustrator. But, he also dreamt of becoming an actor, writer, musician, or even an aviation engineer. He had not considered a career in animation and, in fact, did not even have a precise idea of what animation was.[2]

Yet, he became one of the most influential animation masters in the Soviet Union, an artist who formed in the tradition of classical cel animation only to break the conventions once he turned into a director, a liaison between artists and authorities, a personality who promoted daring films to be created in a society dominated by socialist realism, and a teacher and supporter of young artists that continued to carry on his legacy long after the Soviet empire collapsed.

It all began one day, in May 1937, when Khitruk found himself crossing the threshold of the studio Soyuzmultfilm. His first encounter with the newly founded animation studio was not the most flattering experience. He stepped in the studio with a few of his favorite drawings, but only a quarter of an hour afterwards he was already out. Not only did they not accept him, but they did not even look at his drawings. The director of the studio confirmed that they needed some help but not as an animator, rather as caretaker or plumber![3]

But it was this very refusal that triggered his determination to work at Soyuzmultfilm, "On the way home," he recalls,

> it became clearer and clearer that all my previous dreams – to become a musician, actor, or artist – all these were linked together in one art, and that art seemed to be inaccessible. At that moment, I came to the conviction that I always loved animation and that I was born for it.[4]

NOTES

1   Khitruk graduated in 1936 at the OGIZ art college and then specialized at the Institute of Advanced Studies for Illustrators. Kapkov, *Entsiklopediia otechestvennoi mul'tiplikatsii*, 687. Volkov, "Razgovor o professii," 178.
2   Khitruk, *Professiia-animator*, 2007, 1: 44.
3   Khitruk, 1: 44–45.
4   Khitruk, 1: 45.

Introduction
Khitruk the Man and the Animator

PRE-SOYUZMULTFILM

Born in Tver in 1917, Khitruk was too young to take part in the first experiments of Soviet Animation during the late 1920s. Yet, he was familiar with them, and he often wondered whether Soviet Animation would have developed differently if it continued these experiments instead of turning into a form of art influenced by the American animated films on celluloid sheets.

Soviet animation – unlike its American counterpart which had its roots in comic strips and vaudeville acts – was born from those propaganda posters and caricatures of the 1920s that strongly supported the foundation of the new regime and the new way of life. Soviet animated films harshly criticized any form of capitalism in the form of drawings, cut-outs, or flat marionettes. These techniques limited the movements of the characters, but, as Khitruk says, "it was that very limitation that forced [the animators] to work with creative imagination and find expressive solutions with poor expedients."[1] Most importantly, this method favored the appropriation of the fertile culture of book graphics and illustration of those years, which greatly relied on ground-breaking experimentation in line with principles of modern art.[2] In comparison to the richness of the aesthetic of these films, the cel technique (drawing on transparent celluloid sheets) adopted in the late 1930s seemed to Khitruk to deprive directors of the possibilities to explore new means[3]; it is not by chance that once he became a director, he abandoned traditional cel animation and reverted to cut-out technique.

Khitruk was particularly fascinated by Tsekhanovskii's films *The Post* (*Pochta*, Tsekhanovskii, 1929) and the subsequent *The Tale of the Pope and His Worker Balda* (*Skazka o pope i rabotnike ego Balda*), a never-released film with music composed appositely for it by Dmitrii Shostakovich, of which

DOI: 10.1201/9781003199625-1

only a fragment (the market scene, *Bazaar*) survived. Tsekhanovskii's movies captivated Khitruk with the expressive composition of their frames, which betrayed the influence, already perceived in his book illustrations, of the Soviet avant-garde of the 1920s.[4] Khitruk also appreciated the precise work on the rhythm and editing of Tsekhanovskii's animation, a quality that would become important in his own films.

As the mid-1930s experienced a more rigorous control in Soviet life, the authorities called for a halt to any form of experimentation and for the formation of a centralized studio in Moscow. In 1936, the studio Soiuzdetmul'tfil'm (soon to become Soyuzmultfilm) was created with the goal of focusing on animation for children and following the American successful example in style, technique, and production. The American method of production line and drawing on celluloid sheets had been introduced in Russia already in 1934, when Viktor Smirnov, after returning to Moscow from the American studios of Disney and Fleischer, opened a studio using the same technologies. Smirnov's production of eight films over three years,[5] despite a failing comparison with the American counterpart, showed the possibility of creating entertaining films in a relatively short period of time. The celluloid sheets (introduced in America already in 1914 by Earl Hurd)[6] made it possible to reduce the time in the creation of the films, since it obviated the reproduction of entire drawings on paper for each frame and allowed instead animators to paint the phases of characters' movements on the transparent sheets, which were subsequently juxtaposed onto an unchanged background. Numerous drawings were still necessary to realize the smooth movement of the American style, but the organization of the production in an assembly line proved to be timesaving.

The result, though, was somewhat standardized, in as much as the design of the images would pass under specialized artists in multiple subdivisions before reaching the final stage of production. Also, the Russian animators' inexperience in the new method and the scarcity of resources often led to a flawed emulation of the American films.

A few talented artists tried to oppose the blind adoption of the American style; they saw the process of appropriating a style not based on the domestic visual culture as a threat to the evolution of their own manner; "the dry contour line, more suitable to comics (from which, actually, the first films came out)," Khitruk says, "dictated its aesthetics."[7] Despite the regret felt by some artists about abandoning the early Soviet experiments, the advantages that came with the new technique were evident. Cel drawings allowed a wider flexibility in the plasticity of the movement and greater freedom in relation to the space, and, as Khitruk points out, these were significant aspects that won the debate in favor of a change in direction for animation production.[8] It also helped that this new production system appealed to the Soviet authorities who, at the end of the 1930s, were seeking to exert a greater control over the artists.

In addition, the increased popularity of Disney's films in Russia inexorably contributed to this shift. At the 1935 Moscow International Film Festival, the screening of Mickey Mouse's *The Band Concert* (1935), together with Silly Symphony's *Three Little Pigs* (1933) and *Peculiar Penguins* (1934) enchanted the Russian audience, and Khitruk among them.[9] Artists could not help admiring the cel technique, the attractive use of technicolor, the precise work of synchronization of images with sound and, most strikingly, the detailed elaboration of movement that could convey the distinct personalities of the characters.

The animators at the newly founded Moscow studio would closely analyze not only films by Disney, but also those by Max Fleischer. Among them, Khitruk recalls the *Koko* series of the 1920s and a later film *Popeye the Sailor Meets Ali Baba's Forty Thieves* (1937), which, Khitruk claimed, the animators considered "a kind of Bible."[10] If at first, the early American squash and stretch style (the "macaroni-like" style as they would call it)[11] was appealing for the animators; after the appearance of Disney's long feature films, attention switched to a naturalistic representation of the world, with plenty of details and depth in the background. These films too were studied in detail, in particular the first full-length film *Snow White and the Seven Dwarfs*, made in 1937, just a year after the foundation of Soyuzmultfilm, and, later, *Bambi* (1942), which Khitruk considered "the pinnacle of hand-drawn film art."[12] Taking the films apart and examining closely each scene, frame by frame, was a method that Khitruk himself would adopt when he began to teach.

AT SOYUZMULTFILM

Khitruk ended up at Soyuzmultfilm right at the time when Soviet animation moved toward the new production system and focused on films for children in the hope of replicating the success of Disney's films. Khitruk's first rejection on that May day in 1937 and the failure of a subsequent attempt did not discourage him; on the contrary, the fruitless pursuit strengthened his attachment to his new vocation. Whether it was because he felt a novel attraction to a form of art not yet truly known or simply because of stubbornness, Khitruk decided to take part in a creative contest at Soyuzmultfilm in the fall of 1937. This time, he finally succeeded. Despite competing against older and more experienced artists, Khitruk won a position as an intern and began to work as animator in November 1937.[13]

The first months at Soyuzmultfilm were challenging for a young artist, who, for the first time, tried to navigate the peculiarities of this new artform. Khitruk was a talented artist, and he drew fast – in his childhood he trained for hours at the zoo drawing wolves and monkeys[14] – and, naturally, drawing quickly came as an advantage in a profession where about 15,000 drawings were needed for ten minutes of film. He, however, never truly realized until then that in order to be a good animator, it was not enough to know how to draw but it was also necessary to have some notion of movement and biomechanics, have good hearing and sense of rhythm, and be able to look at the scene with an "inner vision."[15] He needed to instill life to his drawings in the same way as an actor gives life to a character, with an additional step: whereas the actor moves almost instinctively following his emotions and thoughts, the animator has to think of how to convey the inner side of the characters in drawings.[16]

Movement analysis is one of the topics that Khitruk repeatedly approaches in his writings, and which would deserve a separate treatment; it suffices to mention here that at that time, his knowledge of "a feeling of the movement"[17] was not sufficiently refined and Khitruk certainly struggled working on his first assignments. The first task he received was a small scene (four-meter long about eight to ten seconds) in the film *A Little Liar* (*Lgunishka*, Ivanov-Vano, rel. 1941), directed by his first mentor and one of the most experienced directors in the studio, the legendary Ivan Ivanov-Vano (Figure I.1).

In his effort to animate the duckling in Ivanov-Vano's film, Khitruk was frustrated by his character coming out in different forms and sizes and by his failed attempts to connect the drawings into a uniform movement.[18] In addition, the assigned duckling was in his eyes "an extremely bad copy of Donald Duck," on top of which he built up "an even worse, abominable version of it."[19] After three months of helpless attempts, he gave up the scene and, realizing the need for some training, he began to learn by observing the work of other masters. He was particularly fascinated by Boris Dëzhkin, about whom he always talked with great fondness and respect.[20] Behind his back, Khitruk spent hours learning how to express a movement effectively and charge an image with energy.[21]

A pivotal time for Khitruk finally occurred when the animator Faina Epifanova asked him to be her assistant in a scene of Vladimir Suteev's film *The Fly Tsokotukha* (*Mukha-Tsokotukha*, Suteev, rel. 1941). In this film, Khitruk created his first little animated insects, whose appearance on the screen was difficult to discern, but still gave him a much-needed boost of self-confidence.[22]

His first job as an independent animator was an adaptation of a Russian folktale *Ivashko and Baba Yaga* (*Ivashko i Baba-Iaga*, Valentina and Zinaida Brumberg, 1938), followed by a few other films based on national folktales,[23] but it was with another film by Suteev, *Uncle Stëpa* (*Diadia Stëpa*, Bredis, Suteev, 1938), that Khitruk finally began to believe in his ability as an animator and overtake his early struggles in the profession. Khitruk describes the experience of seeing the caretaker he brought to life on the screen as the happiest moment in his professional career.[24] After this film, Khitruk took on few other movies[25] before embarking on a new adventure.

FIGURE I.1 Fëdor Khitruk and Ivan Ivanov-Vano. *Courtesy of Fëdor Khitruk.*

**

At the beginning of 1940, still young and ready for new experiences, Khitruk impulsively left the studio with a couple of fellow animators, Grigorii Kozlov and Boris Titov, for Armenia. In Erevan, the director Lev Atamanov was laying the foundation for an ambitious plan at that time, the creation of the first Armenian full-length animated film, *The Magic Carpet* (*Volshebnyi kover*, rel. 1948, Erevanskaia studiia). Once Khitruk turned up, Atamanov, surprised by his unplanned arrival, gave him only a small job; but the disappointment of not receiving a bigger role did not ruin the experience, Khitruk had fond memories of the time spent in Erevan, including getting married to his colleague Masha Motruk, who followed him from Moscow.[26] When they all returned to Moscow, in May 1941, the studio Soyuzmultfilm welcomed them back. But they worked there no more than a couple of months when the Second World War broke out. With the ongoing war, the priority in film production changed from films for children to shorts addressing topical subjects in the style of satirical posters and propaganda feuilletons. Khitruk, together with other animators and directors, began to work on these short films in between watch-hours on the top of the studio roof during air raids.[27]

Only a few political films appeared in the late 1930s and first years of the war before Soyuzmultfilm was evacuated to Samarkand.[28] Soon Khitruk was called to the army, first as a soldier and before long as a military translator. Khitruk, in fact, knew German quite well, as he lived in Germany with his family for three years during his childhood. His knowledge of German was requested not only at the time of war but also afterwards: as soon as he returned to Moscow at the end of the conflict, he was called back to Berlin as military translator until October 1947.[29]

**

On November 10, 1947, exactly ten years after his first day at the studio, Khitruk stepped back into Soyuzmultfilm. After such a long hiatus, he had to start all over again.[30] As ten years earlier, Dëzhkin patiently assisted Khitruk not only to complete his first assignment – the animation of the elephant hanging above a precipice in *The Elephant and the Ant* (*Slon i muravei*, Dëzhkin, 1948) – but also to understand the fundamentals of animation art.[31] Boris Dëzhkin – a virtuoso of active scenes, with a rare, innate talent for creating dynamic scenes and precise rhythm of movements – became most famous with *An Extraordinary Match* (*Neobyknovennii match*, 1955) and *Old Friends* (*Starye znakomye*, 1956), two films animated by Khitruk, which started a new trend of sport films that would flourish in the following decades and of which Dëzhkin was the absolute master. Khitruk succeeded in animating the personified toys in the films; although, his strength was not so much in the elaboration of active scenes as in the development of the characters' personality. Khitruk's attention to details while conveying the emotional world of his characters made him a widely requested animator in all genres of films produced at Soyuzmultfilm: fables, fairy tales, stories exploring national traditions, adaptations of literary works, and, later, tales set in a contemporary world and parodies of traditional stories.

In several of these films, the depiction of the landscape and especially of the animals living in the woods followed repetitive cliché employed in films of the time, which heavily betrayed the influence of Disney's full-feature films. As in the American films, a painstaking attention to detailed movements often brought animators to rely on the technique of rotoscoping, which involved tracing frame by frame a recording of live-action movement. While this technique helped to reproduce fluid gestures, when used pedantically, it resulted in a slavish emulation of photography, a failed attempt to transpose live-action qualities into animation without considering the imperfect, intangible, and fantastic allure typical of animation.

Despite the occasional overuse of the rotoscope and the frequent adoption of trite solutions, several films made during the late 40s and 1950s were still masterfully done and received many awards within the boundaries of the Socialist bloc and beyond.[32] Some of those films – which turned out to be part of the so-called "Golden Fund" of Russian animation – distinguished themselves by revisiting the aesthetic of famous Soviet book illustrators in the depiction of villages, traditionally decorated izby, folkloric clothing and costumes (a first example of such trend was Ivanov-Vano's successful long-feature film *The Little Humpbacked Horse*, 1947). Their success came doubtlessly from talented artists' crafty attention to details in the elaboration of movement, composition and command of rhythm; but, it was also achieved by the practice at the studio of gathering professionals from different artistic spheres, so that famous and exceptional writers, actors, and composers would join the film team. Besides, the studio system with a strict process for approval, while certainly forcing some ideological control, also required a high level of quality of the films. The Soyuzmultfilm Artistic Council (Khudsovet) was indeed formed by the best artists, and discussions were not only on ideological grounds (a representative of the party was always present at the meetings) but also on solutions toward high-quality aesthetic standards. The constant financing from the state also allowed the directors to focus more on the creation of the film than the funding of the projects. Directors certainly needed to follow deadlines and a budget, but the extent of their involvement in the financial aspect was considerably lighter than that faced by animators after the collapse of the Soviet Union.

As one realizes when looking at the long list of films on which Khitruk worked and all the genres he approached, Khitruk played a considerable role in the flourishing of animation at Soyuzmultfilm, from animator in the first decades, then director, and finally as a teacher. In all his works, he strived to convey the authenticity of fiction through specific details, which, he says, might be overlooked by the spectators, but still act in their subconscious to make the story believable.[33]

It is this very attention to specific details that distinguished Khitruk as a great storyteller and animator. Details, he believed, not only provide hints to the character – see the fox's nonchalant fiddling with her fluffy tail while talking to the duckling in *The Little Grey Neck* (Amal'rik, 1948) – but also help with the rhythm of the story, such as in the film *The Seven-Color Flower* (Tsekhanovskii, 1948), in which the girl delivers her monologue while jumping from one piece of ice to the other, or in *When the Trees Light Up* (Pashchenko, 1950), where the snowman conveys his monologue using Santa Claus's front door as a "partner" (first opening it wide, then, pronouncing the last words while closing it, and lastly, reopening it ajar to add a last word). These details constitute, according to Khitruk, the "dominant," through which the entire scene can be remembered.[34] Much like in Jakobson's definition, the dominant here "rules, determines, and transforms the remaining components."[35] The dominant, though, Khitruk says borrowing from Stanislavsky's method, must be linked to a super-objective (*sverkhzadacha*), "that is," as Stanislavsky says, "the inner essence, the all-embracing goal."[36]

Within the scope of the super-objective imposed by the directors and scriptwriters he worked with – or once a director by himself – Khitruk improvised and developed his characters as an actor would. As he shared talking about the scene with the snowman aforementioned, "the task of entering an image, feeling the character and the state of the character in a concrete situation was the most difficult task, and probably the most interesting for me. I think this is the essence of the work of an animator: he reincarnates twice – he transforms himself in the *typage* [character type] to be animated and through that typage in the character, in the image as in the given script [...] The task of the animator is to embody this image in an emotional movement."[37]

Khitruk worked in the studio Soyuzmultfilm as animator on more than 100 films playing over 200 roles, but only once did he have the rare opportunity to work on a character for the entire film.[38] In these years, at Soyuzmultfilm, it was quite common that characters were animated by various artists. For example, Khitruk recalls how for the award-winning film *Petia and Red Riding Hood* (Stepantsev, Raikovskii, 1958), he animated Petia, Red Riding Hood, the grandma, the wolf and the hunter, but only in the specific episodes assigned to him.[39] The process would usually follow these steps: first, one or more scenarists presented an idea for a character; then, they would pass that specific idea to the art director to be elaborated into a concrete graphic image, a typage, a model; as a last step, animators would give life to this concrete image only in the scenes assigned to them, according to the acting task explained in the director script.

For the film *The Snow Queen* (*Snezhnaia koroleva*, 1957), the director Lev Atamanov opted for a different path and decided to assign Khitruk the entire development of the character Ole Lukøje, a fairy tale gnome borrowed from another story by Hans Christian Andersen ("Ole Lukøje," 1841).

The original typage was created by the talented artist Leonid Shvartsman, who worked on many successful films at Soyuzmultfilm, this character being one of the most famous among those Shvartsman created – it was perhaps surpassed only by the puppet Cheburashka he conceived in the late 1960s. Ole Lukøje's voice, on which Khitruk had to synchronize his acting, was played by the famous MKhAT (Moscow Art Theater) actor Vladimir Gribkov, who delivered his cues in such an expressive tone that Khitruk admitted it was only necessary to listen to the intonation of his voice to guess the gestures and the mimics of the gnome.[40]

Khitruk carefully studied every single detail, from the way the gnome walks trying not to make any noise, to the little gestures that would come naturally from his personality and that would reveal his inner side to the spectator (like candidly blowing his nose after mourning over the destiny of the boy in the story)[41] (Figure I.2).

The gnome's subtle psychological nuances stood out even more when juxtaposed with the character of the Snow Queen (also assigned to Khitruk), whose immobility and cold-heartedness required opposite visual choices.[42] Khitruk's earlier work on a gnome in *The Enchanted Boy* (*Zakoldovannyi mal'chik*, Polkovnikov, Snezhko-Blotskaia, 1955), although still masterfully done, was only a prelude to what he achieved in *The Snow Queen*. On the other hand, the subsequent work of other animators with a different version of the character of Ole Lukøje could not achieve the same level of mastery.[43] Khitruk's work on the gnome narrator is unquestionably one of the best examples of traditional "full animation."[44]

Khitruk most excelled in those films that asked for a thorough character development. As Mikhail Tumelia, one of his students and now well-known director, recalls, Khitruk's strength was in "the lyrical elaboration of a scene with a narrator and the acting out of emotions."[45] Among the innumerable works as animator, the role of Ole Lukøje was probably the one that demonstrated most successfully his mastery and it was certainly Khitruk's favorite.

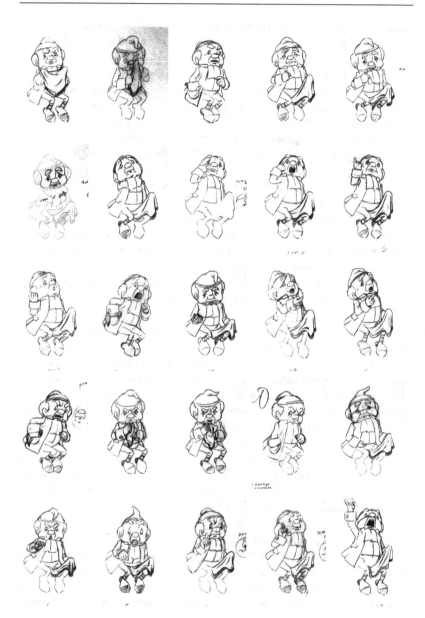

FIGURE I.2 *The Snow Queen*. Ole Lukøje. Key drawings. © Soyuzmultfilm.

NOTES

1 Khitruk, 1: 48–50.
2 Khitruk, 1: 50. For a brief discussion of early Soviet Animation in English see Pontieri, *Soviet Animation and the Thaw*, 6–37.
3 Khitruk, *Professiia-animator*, 2007, 1: 50.
4 Pontieri, Personal Interview with Fëdor Khitruk.
5 Elizarov, *Sovetskaia mul'tiplikatsiia. Spravochnik*, 207; Kapkov, "Viktor Smirnov: ot Disneia k 'Soiuzmul'tfil'mu' i dalee - v zabvenie..."
6 Maltin, *Of Mice and Magic*, 9.
7 Khitruk, *Professiia-animator*, 2007, 1: 50.
8 Khitruk, 1: 50.
9 Khitruk, "Razgovor o professii." In *Mudrost Vymysla*, 178.
10 Khitruk, *Professiia-animator*, 2007, 1: 48.
11 Khitruk, 1: 48.
12 Khitruk, "Razgovor o professii." In *Mudrost Vymysla*. 179. Disney's feature films would be released in Russia after the war, and it was well known among the directors that Stalin particularly liked them. Volkov, "Mul'tiplikatsiia," 117.
13 Khitruk, *Professiia-animator*, 2007, 1: 45.
14 Khitruk, 1: 33.
15 Khitruk, "Razgovor o professii." In Mudrost Vymysla. 179.
16 Khitruk, *Professiia-animator*, 2007, 1: 77.
17 Khitruk, 1: 77.
18 Khitruk, 1: 52.
19 *Animation from A to Z. 7 (Animatsiia ot A do IA. Seriia 7)*
20 Margolina and Liakhovetskii; Khitruk, *Professiia-Animator*, 2007, 1: 53–54.
21 Maliukova, "Fil'm kak bolevoi refleks," 22.
22 Khitruk, *Professiia-animator*, 2007, 1: 56.
23 See a film based on a Buryat contemporary tale *The Hunter Fëdor (Okhotnik Fëdor*, Aleksandr Ivanov, 1938) and an Uzbek folktale *The Tale of the Good Umar (Skazka o dobrom Umar*, Aleksandr Evmenenko, 1938).
24 Khitruk, *Professiia-animator*, 2007, 1: 58. According to Borodin, the film was banned for unclear reasons. Borodin, "Animatsiia podnevol'naia," n.d. Chapter 2, p. 11. However, Sergei Mikhalkov's beloved character of Uncle Stëpa enjoyed screen popularity also in a later film, made in 1964 by Ivan Aksenchuk and the art director Leonid Shvartsman.
25 See for ex. *The Little Cub (Medvezhonok*, Petr Nosov, Ol'ga Khodataeva, Aleksandr Evmenenko, 1940).
26 Khitruk, *Professiia-animator*, 2007, 1: 64–65.
27 Khitruk, 1: 66.
28 See a short list of propaganda films made in these years in Pontieri, *Soviet Animation and the Thaw*, 42–43.
29 Khitruk, *Professiia-animator*, 2007, 1: 68–69.
30 Volkov, "Razgovor o professii," 180.
31 Volkov, 180; Khitruk, *Professiia-animator*, 2007, 1: 70.

32   As Khitruk notes, "the history of the studio as a creative collective and production organism, and ultimately the history of national animation art, does not develop in a straight line. The process of formation of this type of art can be represented as a mountain range or as a cardiogram with ups and downs, and periods of apparent calm, behind which lies the accumulation of strength for the transition to a new quality." Khitruk, "Poniat' dazhe to, chto trudno voobrazit'," 22.

33   Khitruk, *Professiia-animator*, 2007, 1: 180.

34   Khitruk, 1: 96.

35   Jakobson, "The Dominant," 82.

36   Stanislavsky, *Creating a Role*, 65.

37   Khitruk, "Razgovor o professii." In Mudrost Vymysla, 180.

38   Khitruk, *Professiia-animator*, 2007, 2: 146.

39   Khitruk, 2: 146–147.

40   Khitruk, *Professiia-animator*, 2007, 1: 107.

41   Fëdor Khitruk, *Profession Animator*, 1: 107–108.

42   Volkov, "Razgovor o professii," 181.

43   See for ex. the elaboration of the character of Ole Lukøje in a later film, *The Shepherd Girl and the Chimney-Sweep* (*Pastushka i trubochist*, Lev Atamanov, 1965).

44   See discussion of full-animation in Maureen Furniss, *Art in Motion. Animation Aesthetic*, 135–137.

45   Khitruk, *Professiia-animator*, 2007, 2: 267.

A Turning Point in the Profession

1

Story of a Crime (1962), *Man in the Frame* (1966)

FROM ANIMATING TO DIRECTING

After many years spent at Soyuzmultfilm as an animator, Khitruk was ready to make a change in his career. Understanding the different set of tasks required from a director, rather than an animator, he decided to make what he believed to be a radical switch in his profession only when he felt the need to realize his own ideas in a film.[1] He justified this delay in switching to a directorial role with his deep passion for animating characters.[2]

Only while working in the film *Soon There Will Be Rain* (*Skoro idet dozhd'*, Polkovnikov, 1959) did Khitruk have the opportunity to appreciate the directorial position for the first time. Although Polkovnikov fulfilled the role of director, in this film Khitruk oversaw specific episodes, leading and instructing the novel animators; "this was," Khitruk says, "my first real experience of film directing." This experience together with his encounter with talented Czech animators (not only Jiří Trnka, but also Zdeněk Miler, František Vystrčil, Jiří Brdečka, among others) during his trip to Czechoslovakia in 1959 pushed him to explore new paths in his own works.[3]

Even as an experienced director, he tried not to lose touch with his work as animator.[4] This, at times, generated conflicts with talented animators who felt they had limited freedom to create. As Khitruk himself admits,

> the fact that I was an animator interferes in the work as a director. Because I, naturally, play the scene for myself: I see in advance the final result, and that, probably, leads to superfluous dictatorship from my side, so when I work with talented animators, conflicts may arise. [...] Because not only do I explain the task in detail, but I still sketch for myself in advance at least three or four tentative drawings of how it could be developed.[5]

Khitruk was a perfectionist, very demanding of others, but also, and especially, of himself. Although he was not always easy to work with, he was deeply respected for his mastery and for putting heart and soul into his job, always being the first to arrive and the last to leave.[6] He also had a caring attitude, so much so that the younger artists often saw him as a paternal figure.[7] Besides, working in Khitruk's team was unusually stimulating; every film was a masterpiece with its own original solutions, innovatively different from the previous one.[8]

Khitruk's decision to venture into the directorial realm coincided with a peculiar time in the history of the Soviet Union. Starting from the late 1950s the Soviet Union experienced a period of relative détente in the arts thanks to some of the relaxing, although often contradictory, measures taken by Khrushchev.[9] The political context plays an important role in this new phase of animation as, after years of animated films mainly based on fables and folktales and directed exclusively at children, only during the Khrushchev's *Thaw* could Soviet animation finally branch out to target adult audiences, tackle contemporary topics, and introduce innovative styles.[10]

Khrushchev's new directives toward a more open and transparent society led to a revival of satire and a controlled criticism of those flaws of the society that needed to be exposed in order to pursue the goal of "true communism." The 1960s in particular saw a growing interest on satire, but it still seemed a difficult genre to take off in animation. The satirical cinematic newsletter "Diatel" (assigned to the director Evgenii Migunov) was never realized,[11] and the series *Animated Crocodile* (*MUK – Mul'tiplikatsionnyi Krokodil*) did not last long (only a total of six issues in 1960 and 1961).[12] The main challenge in releasing these series on topical issues was linked with the specificities of animation production, which requires a great number of drawings for just a few minutes and consequently a long-time production that would not keep the pace of current events. Their live-action twin project, *Fitil'. An All-Union Satirical Cinematic Journal*, released in 1962, on the other hand, was quite popular and it lasted until 1990. Similarly, another live-action series, this time addressed to children, *Eralash*, would later appear and enjoy a long-lasting success (1974–1996).

A few film-feuilletons came out even earlier, in the second half of the 1950s, but they were still characterized by the same style as previous films for children and on topics that were traditionally accepted (and promoted) by the authorities. *The Sober Sparrow: A Tale for Adults* (*Nep'iushchii vorobei. Skazka dlia vzroslykh*, Amal'rik, 1960), animated by Khitruk, presented the fight over alcoholism in the style of animal fables; *The Signature is Illegible* (*Podpis' nerazborchiva*, A. Ivanov, 1954) dealt with the ineptitude of the managers in allegorical form.[13] Only did *Familiar Pictures* (*Znakomye kartinki*, Migunov, 1957) tackle broader social criticism (such as lack of competence and slackness of workers, dishonesty, and uncultured behavior) rather directly, abandoning the fable convention of animal characters and placing everyday people in a contemporary setting and caricatured style. In this film, instead of detailed phases of the movements and consequent smooth result, the director opted for spare gestures and key drawings. Khitruk's experience while working on this film as animator, as Mikhailin notices, became invaluable while searching for stylized character movements in his first directorial film *Story of a Crime*.[14]

The discussion about the need to address topical themes and explore new styles was quite alive throughout the 1950s. Directors' articles appeared in the press, especially in the highly regarded cinema journal *Iskusstvo kino*, and expressed the desire to expand animation to include satirical films, address contemporary topics and create original films thematically and aesthetically. They also condemned the conveyor-like production, which was seen as limiting the artists' original creative choices to pre-approved clichés and standard solutions.[15] Directors also expressed the need to take into consideration the very specificity of animation, avoid a mere copy of reality, and hence eschew the so-called "naturalism" promulgated in the studio.[16] Three films released almost at the same time answered these demands to varying degrees, *The Bathhouse* (*Bania*, Karanovich, Yutkevich, 1962), *Great troubles* (*Bol'shie nepriiatnosti*, Zinaida and Valentina Brumberg, 1961), and, most importantly, Khitruk's *Story of a Crime* (*Istoriia odnogo prestupleniia*, 1962).

The Bathhouse brings back the satirical and agitational tradition of Mayakovsky through a new stylized way of representing the setting, the city, and the characters, as well as an innovative use of a combination of puppets, drawings, and live action footage. *Great Troubles*, instead, explores the theme of parasitism, corruption, and the phenomenon of *stiliagi* in a style that exploits the conventionalities of children's drawings.[17] But it is with Khitruk's

Story of a Crime that a more definitive innovative and influential step was undertaken in Soviet animation. As the director Stanislav Sokolov comments,

> Khitruk sensed his time, it was a time of changes in society that brought necessary changes in art. They could not continue to work in a conventional way, they needed a new language; and Khitruk appeared just at the right time.[18]

If *Story of a Crime* fostered a production of more films addressed to adults, it also opened the gate to a different approach to animation. The experimentation in style that this film introduced eventually pervaded many films, not only those for adults with topical themes, but also films based on traditional children's stories, the best of which, once more were directed by Khitruk.

The search for an original style, a form that would inextricably fit the content, was a process that propelled the making of each of Khitruk's films and was a revolutionary concept at the time. Experimental searches meant a disruption of the studio system and the creation of smaller workshops which favored what had been called by many critics "authorial animation," a kind of animation that would elude standardized choices adopted in big studios and emphasize the individual style of the artist. As in any revolutionary phases in art, however, a profound knowledge of the tradition must be the foundation against which the new phase reacts. Khitruk's mastery lies in his deep knowledge of the traditional cel animation adopted at the studio and the foundation of animation art. His skills shone in the expressiveness of the drawing, the significance of each gesture, the sense of rhythm of a scene and of the entire film, the ear for the right sound, and most dearly to Khitruk, the ability to condense a feeling, an emotion, or a situation in telling details. When he met a young artist, Sergei Alimov, with a novel and original way to approach animation, Khitruk could channel his knowledge onto new paths. From this collaboration the revolutionary *Story of a Crime* broke through.

STORY OF A CRIME (ISTORIIA ODNOGO PRESTUPLENIIA, 1962)[19]

The effect of *Story of a Crime* in the studio was explosive. Although signs of innovation timidly surfaced already at the end of the 1950s, this film combined both ground-breaking style and novelty in themes. It reflected the desire to approach animation not only as entertainment for children, but also as a form of art that could reflect contemporary society and express an era that seemed to promise some liberalization in the arts.

Inspired by his personal experience,[20] Khitruk prepared a draft with few ideas for a script that the studio passed on to none other than Mikhail Vol'pin.[21] In Vol'pin's hands the script gave life to the story of how a simple accountant, Mamin, a good and meek citizen, driven by the unconcerned noise and behavior of "uncultured" (*nekul'turnye*) neighbors, ends up killing the two noisy caretakers that wake him up early in the morning. The story was told with Vol'pin's typical wit, subtle satire, and humor.

Vol'pin was one of the few, if not the only, experienced members of the team: Khitruk was debuting his role of director with this film, the art-director Alimov was finishing the VGIK (the renowned Moscow State School of Cinematography), and also the cameramen and the animators had just finished their courses.[22] They were young and not conditioned by the traditional animation endorsed in the studio; they wanted to "turn their film into a bomb!"[23] And they certainly did.

The creative team ideally combined Khitruk's experience in classical animation, and the young artists' challenging attitude against traditional art. The enthusiastic animators brought in an innovative wave that was common among the young generation of students of the second half of the 1950s, a time that marked a turning point in the social and cultural life of the Soviet Union. As Gromov comments, his students at the VGIK often rebelled against the teachers' insistence on the study of classical and dogmatic works and hungered for being exposed to new styles and art from different traditions inside and outside the country. They could see a few of those "seditious" pictures at the Tretyakov Gallery, at the Pushkin State Museum of Fine Arts, or the Hermitage in Leningrad, and they also were exposed to different works while studying at the VGIK. However, several of the most traditional teachers as well as the adopted textbooks still tended to avoid the discussions of modern art.[24]

Socialist realism in art was still the mandatory policy. It required a depiction of reality that would reflect the development of socialism and a positive attitude toward the socialist world. The graphic arts of the 1940s and 1950s promoted a form that best represented the socialist realist canon and made any less-than-ideal representation of life, or any deformation, that is any attempt of detachment from the accepted norm, an "aesthetic crime."[25] The student generation of the late 1950s and 1960s strived to find a new conventionality that would reflect the changing time. Among them, Alimov was ready to break with these traditions in visual arts as well as in animation. When called to collaborate at Soyuzmultfilm, he brought with him the same challenging attitude he had at the VGIK; it was time to introduce new styles also in traditional Soviet animation.

Innovation of Style

Khitruk's first sketches were made following long-established aesthetics – the city arranged in traditional perspective, the characters in the habitual naturalistic style. The director, though, felt that the world he created lacked something fundamental that prevented him from moving ahead.[26] Only when Sergei Alimov showed the director his drawings did Khitruk have a revelation.[27] The pictures presented a contemporary style, very angular and sharp, which strikingly departed from the mainstream round traits and soft lines, and cunningly suited the satirical tone adopted in the film. The geometric angularity of the images brought animation closer to graphic art and caricature and made it take upon itself their task of criticizing and ridiculing contemporary society while addressing the public in a straightforward way; "the film acquired that detachment from the details of everyday life, that poignancy that I was looking for," Khitruk says.[28]

This direct and concise style, as well as the use of cut-outs, recalls early Soviet animated films. The jerky movements typical of the technique contrast with the fluid gestures of the cel animation adopted by Soyuzmultfilm, especially in the cases when the rotoscope was overused. In *Story of a Crime*, though, the lack of fluidity in the characters' movements does not derive from primitive means, as in early animation, rather it responds to the general principle of maximal meaningfulness in concise expression. Characters are now depicted in a stylized manner, movements are reduced to key, essential phases, backgrounds are stripped to expressive details, and the use of collages and split-screen allows a representation of reality on multiple levels.

The way of representing characters and backgrounds in 'limited animation,' i.e., in an economical way, with simplified movements and details, followed a worldwide reaction against Disney's traditional 'full animation' style which reigned in the animation world for decades.[29] The 1950s saw artists detaching from the American big studio's conveyor-system and its strict subdivision of labors and opening smaller independent studios, in which they searched for new ways of representing the world in animation. Khitruk was most influenced by the American UPA films as well as the Czech studio Bratři v triku, from where he recollects a poster with a motto that summarized the new trend: "minimum of means and maximum of expression."[30] A similar laconic style also characterized the ex-Yugoslavian Zagreb School, although both Khitruk and Alimov admitted in personal interviews[31] that they were influenced by the Zagreb school later on (see Khitruk's *The Island*, made in 1973). Despite being depicted in a highly simplified manner, the characters in limited animation were more expressive because they appeared, in the director John Halas's words, "more in tune with the concept of design and stylized humor in the stories, and better integrated with their equally stylized backgrounds."[32]

Alimov followed the path of many of his colleagues abroad searching for aesthetic choices that would exploit the conventionality of the drawings instead of relying on those perfect movements and camera-wise effects that characterized Disney's "cinematic approach."[33] Alimov and Khitruk aimed for visual choices that would underline the specificity of animation, which turns drawings into an "aesthetic imprint of reality."[34] According to Khitruk, this allowed a certain freedom in elaborating images in a plastic way, that is, the animator did not have to reproduce the entire sequence of actions, but could skip the usual links and present the scene in the most laconic form, leaving the spectator the freedom to fill in the gaps.[35] In his work as animator Khitruk refined key gestures in details, always striving for verisimilitude; in this film, instead, he distilled the gestures in merely one laconic movement that would convey the key to the entire scene or reveal the hero's character (see for example Mamin's movement before sitting on the chair in Figure 1.1).[36]

The same laconic effect is achieved in the mass scenes: the mass seems to be licked off the subway platform, the walking crowd is revealed through their flickering legs, faces suddenly pop in around the crime scene (and pop out when the story reverses in time). This economical and essential way of portraying the masses gains a mechanical quality that fits the overall tendency toward modern concepts of rationality and functionality which were perceived as congruent with contemporary life. The dynamism of modern times transpires through a representation of what David MacFadyen defines as "blocks of nervousness," realized with "flat chromatic blocks stylized in accelerated, jerky motions."[37] The "flat chromatic blocks" express in a limited palette and contrasting colors not a mimetic representation of reality but a distilled reality. Color here fulfills the function sought by Eisenstein in a

FIGURE 1.1 *Story of a Crime.* Mamin. Character's details. © Soyuzmultfilm.

cartoon: "The key principle consists in separating colors from what necessarily lies beneath it, to draw it out into a general feeling, and make this general feeling become a subject again."[38]

The modern design principles of patches of solid color, together with schematic drawings, clear geometric lines, skewed perspective, poster-like style, and flat figures deprived of shadows accentuate the flattening-out effect of the figures (Figures 1.2 and 1.3). By emphasizing the two-dimensionality of the sketches, the animators also underlined the very specificity of their own artistic medium, the flat surface on which a drawing is traced.[39]

The flat figures in the film become conventional signs able to convey with a minimum of traits a general characteristic.[40] They become "types" easily recognizable by the audience, like masks in the *Commedia dell'arte*, or the *typage* of Eisenstein's tradition. Each character embodies a trait of "uncultured" behavior against which the figure of Mamin is juxtaposed. In elaborating the protagonist's image, Khitruk and Alimov had in mind a Chaplinesque hero armed with both tragic and comic sides.[41] However, while Chaplin stands out from the surroundings with his exaggerated gestures and

FIGURE 1.2 *Story of a Crime.* Stylized representation of space. © Soyuzmultfilm.

FIGURE 1.3   *Story of a Crime.* Flattening out effect. © Soyuzmultfilm.

costume, Mamin's quiet demeanor and ordinary clothing is hardly notice-able. If Chaplin's costume constitutes one of the main elements of his mask, Mamin's clothing is purposely chosen to identify an ordinary man of the 1960s. The style and fabric used for the clothes for both Mamin and the masses were fashionable and easily recognizable; even more so as they were cut out from the pages of magazines of the time and rearranged by Alimov in a collage form.[42]

Notwithstanding the difference in appearance, Mamin still shares with Chaplin the anti-hero stock-type, a victim of increasingly challenging situa-tions which provoke a comic reaction and, at the same time, elicit a sense of compassion and sympathy from the spectator. Not only Chaplin's type-mask but also his expressive pantomime influenced and fascinated Khitruk and Alimov.[43] Pantomime is the foundation of films like *Story of a Crime*, in which lack of words and the conventionalized representation of space render the movement paramount – it is not by chance that Khitruk studied in detail the work not only of Chaplin, but also of the famous French mime Marcel Marceau. Whereas Marceau played with an invisible space, Mamin moves in a space reduced to a minimum: the staircase between the building's floors is practically non-existent, and only a little colored square on a black back-ground defines Mamin's apartment.

A Play with Languages

The paradox of the film lies in that the entire film pivots on sound, but it lacks words. Not by chance, "Silence" ("Tishina") was the original title of Mikhail Vol'pin's script.[44] The rare spoken lines in the film call for a humorous response to either verbal puns or parody of clichés of official speech. Thus, at the shout "Stoite!" ("stop"/"stand up"), the polysemantic value of the word materializes on screen – everyone stops and the two women (supposedly dead) stand up; or later, the officer's words "Let's turn the wheel of history" shifts the official speech into the parody of detective films' clichés.

The rest of the film plays with different kinds of language with similar comic effect. Whenever the characters in the film establish an act of communication where dialogue would normally be used as a code for the exchange of information, the conversation is presented not through a verbal, but a musical code. During a confrontation, once more around loud noise, a sweet clarinet sound substitutes Mamin's voice, whereas a boastful trombone reproduces the rude neighbor's voice. In another scene, the music from Mamin's neighbor completely drowns out Tatiana's speech in the *Evgenii Onegin* film on TV he is watching[45] (Figure 1.4).

FIGURE 1.4   *Story of a Crime*. TV Scene. © Soyuzmultfilm.

Here, the switch of codes is heightened by the juxtaposition of animation and real live-action projected on TV. Instead of perceiving the languages of the image and the spoken word as a single-language phenomenon (see Lotman's discussion of the one-language phenomenon, *odnoiazychnyi fenomen*, in film),[46] the image disassociates itself from the sound, and the two languages are separated. In this process of substitution, the audience perceives a violation of norms, Shklovskian estrangement is created, the "shape" of the work is foregrounded, and a comic result is achieved.[47]

Sound effects, on the other hand, are reproduced with documentary credibility throughout the film, but they are still manipulated to create an increasingly wittier outcome.[48] The level of noise somewhat diminishes, just as the reaction of Mamin intensifies; the climax resolves into a materialized metaphor, one "last drop" of a leaking faucet triggers his homicidal thoughts.

The theme of sound also manifests in a symbolic representation of space, in which no precise boundaries define the area around Mamin. His world is presented with no borders, as though he has no right to be detached from society. The striving of the individual of the 1960s to carve an autonomous place from the ideology of the mass is here frustrated by a representation of space that does not allow the individual to be depicted as a simple and independent entity.[49]

His space is open, visible, and often depicted in the filmic frame together with other spaces not belonging to him. Simultaneous montage realized with a split screen presents contemporaneous actions, taking place in different spaces; two shots are spliced together in a relation of simultaneity, and at the same time cause and effect (Figure 1.5).

The conception of split-screen technique goes back to early cinema, and it is a device that always fascinated Khitruk even in later years (see for ex. his ideas for *A Day Before Our Era*). In *Story of a Crime*, behind its implications on a thematic level, it is used with the specific purpose of reorganizing the space in the most efficient way for dramatic purpose and comic effect; it is a form of narrative condensation in limited representation of space.

By introducing spatial relations not in a naturalistic way, but rather in a stylized manner, the director leaves the audience with the task of creating the missing links, a process that often comes subconsciously in the mind of the spectator. The space is fragmented and consists of parts put together almost like in a collage; the elements maintain their significance in their original realm and at the same time they must be read in terms of their function within the whole. The process cannot but echo the constant negotiation in the film between the individual and the overall society.

FIGURE 1.5 *Story of a Crime.* Split Screen. © Soyuzmultfilm.

A Move from Socialist Realism

The film offers a picture of everyday life a spectator could relate to, an honest representation of a contemporary society that displays conflicts within itself. It is not the ideal world promulgated by socialist realism, but a collective composed of people violating those norms of social order and rules of shared behavior that go under the category of *kul'turnost'*, seen, in Catriona Kelly's words, as a "force for stability and homogeneity"[50] connected to "a dream of harmonious integration."[51] Mamin, on the other hand, represents an exception to the general attitude of the people around him. He is depicted as the proper Soviet man: he is nice to children and polite to his fellow men, opens doors for people, offers his seat in the subway, observes the rules, and is dedicated to his work. The paradoxical result is that *kul'turnost'* in this film is represented by a man who commits a crime.[52]

By having the ideal character transgress, the directors undermine the boundary between right and wrong. In the film there is no distinction between a criminal deed and uncultured behavior; both are deviations that need to be corrected. The crime Mamin commits, although blameworthy, attacks those people who threaten an officially ideal harmonic system with their daily uncultured behavior. The character's act, however, is not driven by any socially edifying ideals; in this, Mamin radically differs from the heroes of the socialist realist canon. He does not react with the aim of exhorting others to mend their ways, nor does he seem to be interested in socializing with others but intervenes only when people's behavior interferes with his privacy and violates his personal space.

The film also reverses the relationship between the individual and society as shown in a typical socialist realist canon. In the traditional Soviet novel, the hero who deviates from the norms imposed by society gradually becomes aware of his mistakes; as he evolves, he achieves ideological consciousness, eventually repents for his misconduct and in doing so, he gains acceptance by society.[53] Character development according to these rules can also be found in many Soviet films animated by Khitruk usually in a form suitable for children's education: The child commits a mistake, repents the bad deed, and consequently is accepted back into society, with his family and friends around him.[54]

In *Story of a Crime*, a different process occurs. The character commits a crime and thereby violates the rules of society, but the spectator does not witness his repentance. Instead, the film presents a reversal of time and focuses on the events that preceded the criminal act. This subtle device challenges the official canon by eliding altogether the phase of repentance, as well as by pressing a society that is far from ideal to recognize its share of the guilt. At the end, the film finishes with words that stress the sharing of responsibility for the crime among the crowd, but at the same time underline the need to punish the transgression: "Who is really guilty, comrades? A crime occurred and Vasilii Vasil'evich will certainly be arrested. But we hope that the people who decide the fate of the citizen V. V. Mamin will see our film and will understand everything."

The last sentence in the film is clearly self-reflexive. The narrator draws the viewers' attention to the film itself and to the function of the film. This moment of self-reflection raises more general issues, such as the question of the role of the arts in society and the messages conveyed by the mass media. It also presents an opportunity to consider the different messages proposed to the masses during the Stalin era and in these Thaw years. The banal conclusion with an edifying speech directed to the characters in the film (but at the same time to each spectator), a speech pronounced by a figure of unimpeachable authority, is a device found in many endings of Soviet films. Khitruk inserted a moral ending, yet in this last version of the film he reaches a compromise – a criminal is declared guilty, but the community shares its part of the responsibility.[55] No repentance is shown from either side; in the very last scene a trunk makes its appearance with a load of junk that, with an amplified noise, is dumped in the courtyard.

The Soviet Union of the 1960s[56]

In portraying the typical day of a simple citizen, Khitruk and Alimov place the character in a recognizable Moscow environment. The spectator realizes that the story takes place in Moscow not from traditional elements of concretization[57] such as monuments or tourist attractions, but from small, specific details. Geographic concretization actualizes through everyday life details and the depiction of the streets, buildings, courtyards, as well as the subway's swinging doors, vaulted platforms, long escalators, and rows of seats packed with passengers immersed in their reading.

Collages place the film into a specific spatial-temporal reality. Fragments from contemporary newspapers, magazines, and posters function as synecdochic representations of papers read by the characters, movie advertisements, and announcements hung on the office wall; while real photographs of buildings and streets provide a picture of the city as seen from the windows of Mamin's office. This material underlines the sense of a specific locus in time and provides ground for satirizing a particular moment in Soviet reality. The spectators' recognition and identification with the contemporary world contributed to the comic effect, but in rare cases it sparked indignation for what was considered a sign of irreverence toward the system.[58]

Indeed, a subtle parody of Soviet policies and discourse appears in the film, but it is always presented in a comic tone, such as in the scene in which a big banner pinned to the wall of Mamin's office exhorts the employees to fulfil the year's plan three days earlier with the slogan, "Let's fulfil this year's plan by December 28!" (Figure 1.6).

This incitement to complete the plan three days early sounds like a mockery of the communist year planning in light of the widely promulgated effort to fulfil five-year plans in fewer years. The comic effect is emphasized by the juxtaposition of an idealistic commitment to accomplish ambitious plans in the name of the progress of the country, with the real contemporary world, where, under the above-mentioned sign, people are idling away their time. In more than one scene of the film the director hints at the widespread tendency toward absenteeism and apathy: people in the office are portrayed just talking and smoking instead of working, and at five o'clock when Mamin leaves the office, everyone has already left.[59] Similarly, throughout the film, posters inviting citizens to behave properly are shown next to people breaking the same rules to provide other examples of parody of official propaganda discourse.

Another reference to a distinctive Soviet context – Khrushchev's vast building projects aimed to ease the country's serious and urgent housing problem – concretizes in the image of the construction of a house in front of Mamin's window. A visual comic gag is at the base of this scene, the house is built very quickly with all the necessary accessories (a chair, a cat,

ВЫПОЛНИМ ГОДОВОЙ ПЛАН К 28 ДЕКАБРЯ !

FIGURE 1.6 *Story of a Crime.* Propaganda banner. Cel. © Soyuzmultfilm.

a plant, laundry hung up, curtains, etc.) and on the top of the last block is a sign that reads, "Save your money in the state bank." The housing question is posed from different points of view. There is a movement from macrocosm to microcosm, from a grandiose project to its practical effects on daily life. The scene begins with a panoramic shot of a landscape full of houses and rotary cranes, which emphasizes the vastness of the building project (Figure 1.7).

From this point of view, the city looks like a conglomerate of buildings hanging in the air: "it looked not just as architectural compositions, but had a figurative, anthropomorphic characterization; they became like little worlds," says Khitruk.[60] From a narrower point of view, through Mamin's office window, the construction of the apartment building progresses block by block at the rhythm of the hero's typing as to suggest that it is with the honest activity of workers such as Mamin that the country is moving forward (Figure 1.8).Finally, inside Mamin's apartment, the noise heard from the neighbors is the ultimate sign of the poor quality of the building.

In earlier versions of the script, more obvious and direct allusions to the inadequate conditions of the new houses were revised to tone down the criticism[61]; yet, the disapproval of the poor quality of the buildings comes forth, especially in the scene in which the loud noise from upstairs shakes Mamin's walls. The criticism was inevitably unwelcomed inside the

FIGURE 1.7 *Story of a Crime.* Panoramic view of buildings under construction. © Soyuzmultfilm.

FIGURE 1.8 *Story of a Crime.* Construction from Mamin's window. © Soyuzmultfilm.

Artistic Council, "The shaking of the ceiling is annoying. It suggests that the construction is of poor quality. In general it is necessary to place the main stress on the fact that norms of social order are not being observed."[62] Despite some resistance, this scene was not cut out but was instead exploited to achieve a comic effect.

The atmosphere at the Council reflected the general climate of the Thaw, where conservative and liberal positions were often in confrontation with one another. Khitruk's film cunningly played with both stances, trying to navigate the complex relations within the establishment, that is between the authorities and the audience on the one hand, and the authorities and the artists on the other.

Petrushevskaya elucidates Khitruk's diplomatic position:

> In Russia there has always been what you could call a mafia of 'decent people.' It is still active today. This might sound crazy, but somewhere up there were the Party, the Communists, the government, the KGB, the militia, the *Druzhina*. And we were down here. Khitruk fought to ensure that Norstein got a state award. If Norstein hadn't received that award, *Tale of Tales* would probably have remained banned until 1986. Norstein would not have had a chance if Khitruk had not been so involved. That's how the mafia of the decent people worked. And in the sphere of animation Khitruk was the ringleader.[63]

Khitruk was raised in the Soviet regime, fought for his country, and was a member of the Communist party. But he also saw the weaknesses of the regime and desired to 'lay them bare' in his films. At times, some of his criticism aligned with the same promulgated by the authorities, but even in these cases, his films were not dry propaganda works, rather reflections and criticism on society with a will of reconciling his own beliefs and wishes with reality.

Production and Reception of the Film

Khitruk opted for a representation of the weaknesses of society in a light satirical way, rather than a moralizing manner. In the Soviet Union, though, satire always played a dangerous role, toeing the border of the admissible. While it is considered a good means for criticism of the weaknesses of society, it is also a mode that reveals the existence of these faults and was generally allowed in the Soviet Union only insofar as the criticism could be manipulated by the dominant ideology. Whenever satire slips out of control, it turns into an undesired (for the authorities) criticism of the system. With Khrushchev's relative openness toward satire as a "corrective tool" in the fight against social ills, satire experienced a revival and a few satirical animated films reappeared in these years. It seems that in the Soyuzmultfilm studio, the members of the Artistic Council were aware of the danger and expressed contrasting positions, some of them progressive, some quite orthodox. The entire approach to Khitruk's film was one of caution.

Contrary to the custom of showing new films openly to the entire studio, the directors decided to limit the screening of *Story of a Crime* to a small group of people; "after all it was not a children's tale, but a satirical feuilleton, a risky and little-known genre."[64] The screening took place in absolute silence and no comments followed; Khitruk's team thought their film was an utter failure:

> The screening passed in complete silence – not a laugh, not a reaction. I had disappointments in my life, but never like this. And not only me, but the entire group was also depressed. I remember that while we left the room, one of the animators asked for the permission to re-do one scene and I replied: 'Lesha, not a scene, but we would need to reshoot the entire film!'[65]

Then they showed the film to the entire studio. The room was full. There were some expectations, overblown by the administration's early decision of not allowing an open screening, but this time, the film provoked a completely different reaction. From the very beginning of the film, there were bursts of applause – something that would happen quite rarely at the in-studio screenings – and laughs did not cease till the end. It was a success. Khitruk's team could now settle, but the nervous tension they endured during this screening would find an image in a later film (*Film Film Film*, 1968) (Figure 1.9).

FIGURE 1.9   *Film Film Film*. Sketch for final scene. © Soyuzmultfilm.

Story of a Crime was released and achieved great resonance with both public and press, to the point that it generated talks about a sequel with the same character and new adventures. But Khitruk did not want to continue the story of Mamin, he was ready to move on, "for us the theme was exhausted, we were interested in opening new doors."[66]

FROM CRITICISM TO HARSH SATIRE. *MAN IN THE FRAME* (*CHELOVEK V RAMKE*, FËDOR KHITRUK, 1966)[67]

After *Story of a Crime*, Khitruk switched to films for children, *Toptyzhka* and *Bonifatius's Vacation* (more in the next chapter), but soon he felt the need to tackle topical issues again. This time he narrowed his target to a particular sphere of society, the bureaucratic world. Attacks against the bureaucrats dated back to Lenin's time and regularly appeared in satirical journals. *Man in the Frame*, however, does not stop at mild criticism, but rather presents a dark picture of the bureaucrat and of the system itself.

Character, Space and Literary References

Man in the Frame focuses on the depiction of a "situation" more than the unfolding of events; all actions pivot on the ascent of a man on the career ladder and its detrimental effect on the surrounding world. The visual choice adopted by Khitruk and, once more, the art director Sergei Alimov, is the literalization in concrete form of the Russian metaphor of the "paper man" (*bumazhnyi chelovek*). The character is created piece by piece on paper: with every line typed in the Employee Personal Record Form, a fragment of his face materializes, until a full portrait forms (Figure 1.10).

As in Tynianov's Lieutenant Kizhe,[68] Khitruk's character seems to exist only on paper, and as does the fictitious Kizhe, he freely races to the highest ranks. The character's grotesque, almost surreal image adds a dark tone to any reference to the real bureaucratic world. His depiction on a flat paper-like surface emphasizes his emptiness, as his lack of a real face reflects the absence of a soul – in the funeral scene, his grotesque and empty face is revealed behind a removable set of glasses comprised of eyes and tears (Figure 1.11).

The bureaucrat's narrowmindedness materializes in the spatial organization: his frame of mind is literally rendered by a small picture frame

FIGURE 1.10 *Man in the Frame.* Form with negations. © Soyuzmultfilm. Subtitles Films by Jove.

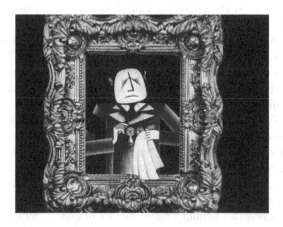

FIGURE 1.11 *Man in the Frame.* Removable glasses with tears. © Soyuzmultfilm.

in which he is enclosed. His world is limited, sealed, and separated from the life that surrounds him. Like Chekhov's "Man in the Case,"[69] Khitruk's character isolates himself from the rest of the world and oppresses the surroundings with his presence and obtuse refusal of any form of lively life. But if Belikov lives with the fear of everything that surrounds him and fights for affirming a safe, in his view, world, the bureaucrat in the frame is driven not by fear but by ambition and desire of power. The frame is his secure space, the tool that allows his ascent. It is, as Khitruk says, "what makes a person the way he is, what symbolizes the very social status of the person, and together with it his character."[70] Khitruk and Alimov looked for frames "which spoke in the most picturesque way about luxury, about the importance of the works contained in them," says Khitruk, "This, perhaps, was the idea-image – the frame was a visual image of a person in society."[71] The frame itself gradually becomes a character in its own right – it moves and changes shape, participates in the events depicted, gradually enslaves the bureaucrat, and ultimately swallows him.

Alimov's graphic style eschews a naturalistic representation of reality; instead, it is more oriented toward the grotesque.[72] His manner shows a personal elaboration of the eclectic styles he favored, from the grotesque and sharp figures of German expressionism to the dynamic compositions of contemporary life typical of the OST (Obshchestva stankovistov – The Society of Easel Artists); from Picasso's fragmented figures to the phantasmagoric compositions of the surrealists.

Cut-out figures and geometric forms move on screen in a deliberately mechanical way, which underlines the machine-like driving force that lies behind the character and reduces him to a puppet, or rather, to an automaton, deprived of all feelings or scruples. The language spoken by the character is made up of monosyllables or mere agglomerations of letters that are void of any meaning, as bureaucratic language often is.

Like a mechanical puppet, the character ascends in his career, ignoring all distractions. External events, temptations, and emotions fail in making him capitulate; rather, they have the opposite effect of strengthening the bureaucrat's constricting frame. The way the character is depicted is very static – as he is confined inside his frame for the entire film – but Alimov is able to convey his essential personality through simple hand gestures, or slight movements of head and eyes. A look at Alimov's drawings, illustrations, as well as preparatory sketches for his animated films[73] confirms his mastery in conveying with simple traits, expressive poses, and peculiar compositions, an entire story within a single frame. This ability made him not only a talented animation artist but also an exceptional illustrator of children's books.

Real Life in Still Photographs

In the first scene of *Man in the Frame*, "Meeting with Life" (*Vstrecha s zhizn'yu*), Khitruk juxtaposes Alimov's flat drawn image of the character with a series of still photographs depicting those aspects of society from which the character isolates himself. Festive street demonstrations, sporting activities, smiling women, and happy children appear on the screen. Among the people portrayed, a little girl skipping rope will become a recurrent motif throughout the film, a sign of vitality that sharply contrasts with the main character's static and almost lifeless activity. Not only are photographs arranged in a visual counterpoint evoking lessons from Soviet montage, but also each single frame is organized according to what Eisenstein would call a "conflict inside the frame" (*vnutrikadrovyi konflikt*), that is, a conflict in the graphic direction of the lines formed by the subject in the frame, a conflict of planes, of volume and space,[74] which conveys a sense of the dynamic and lively world that surrounds the inactive bureaucrat.

There is no live-action cinematic footage, but quick editing of static images achieves an effect similar to that of Eisenstein's famous marble lion rising to its feet in *The Battleship Potemkin* (*Bronenosets "Potemkin,"* 1925). The director creates a sense of movement using a series of photographs presented with slightly changed angles, different colors, or through panning camera movements, which focus on close-ups of various details, or reveal in long shots a bigger picture.

Workers could not be absent in the depiction of an active society. The images of healthy and smiling workers are set up in opposition to Khitruk's bureaucrat, who merely sits at a desk, signing and stamping papers or simply passing files from one hand to another. The accusation of "lack of productivity" inherent in the depiction of the character resounded as a harsh criticism in a society where "parasites" were severely blamed and punished.[75] Khitruk manipulates Soviet propaganda in a way that some of its principles are used to promote an ideal life and, at the same time, attack its weaknesses; his position is not open dissent, rather criticism within a communist realm.

As per Soviet tradition, workers are mostly depicted in all their powerful glory against an open horizon or sky, making them a symbol of all the workers who contribute to the prosperity of the country. The people and their jobs are represented in a continuum, as an inseparable entity, parts of a larger vision of life. There are no delimiting frames around them; the ultimate image of the fusion of the person with the surrounding space is a picture of a doctor in his white smock and surgical mask, whose edges merge with the white background – workers and environment become one. The reverse situation occurs in the fictional space created in the film's animated sequences; the frame becomes increasingly bigger and thicker, delimiting the character and separating him from the surrounding world.

Character's Isolation from Society

Love, friendship, fantasy, and freedom – all represented in the film in symbolic forms – are feelings and states that the bureaucrat lets pass by without being touched by them. As a symbol of love and beauty, an image from the Renaissance, Botticelli's *Venus*, appears on the screen (Figure 1.12).

The Renaissance image is an iconic sign of harmony and pure beauty, of an idealized world in opposition to the pragmatic and aseptic environment of the bureaucrat. In the collage that appears on the screen, the harmonious traits and sinuous lines that delineate the Venus contrast with the sketchy, straight, and simplified lines of the character in the frame. The image of Venus is cut out from the environment in which she belongs in Botticelli's painting and shares the frame with the character. No borders delimit her space, her boundless and eternal force is conveyed through a color that fills in the entire film frame and turns the white, black, and grey sterile paper world of the bureaucrat into a pinkish-purple field. To approach beauty would require the bureaucrat to step out of his enclosed space, but he refuses to venture into this world without boundaries; therefore, the background of the film frame returns to an austere paper white, and the frame is restored.

FIGURE 1.12 *Man in the Frame.* The man and Venus. © Soyuzmultfilm.

FIGURE 1.13   *Man in the Frame.* The kite breaks the space. © Soyuzmultfilm.

On only one more occasion does a sign from the outside world (this time in the form of a kite) break into the grey world of the bureaucrat. The futile attempt is quickly dismissed. No signs of freedom or fantasy are allowed in the character's world – the bureaucrat folds the kite into the shape of one of his documents and passes it on (Figure 1.13).

Even in this revised shape, the kite is dangerous and provokes the fall of another bureaucrat who holds it in his hands; our hero, instead, refusing to follow the same destiny, throws the remnant of the kite in the garbage, and rises up a notch in the hierarchy.

From a Study of the Human Soul to an Attack to the System

This film does not limit itself to the disapproval of a single bureaucrat's behavior, but becomes an expression of more universal values, about "a person's responsibility towards society."[76] In general, in his films Khitruk is more concerned with the study of the human soul and the place of the individual in society than expressing a political statement. "When making *Man in the Frame*," Khitruk says,

> I was primarily concerned with moral and social problems. I wanted to challenge not only bureaucratic indifference but also the petty egoist in

every one of us. We wanted the viewers to understand that pursuit of a comfortable job and status often deprives one of kindness, magnanimity, and compassion. A man becomes a soulless career-seeker.[77]

There is a scene, however, that can be read not only as an expression of ultimate *podlost'* derived by careerism and cowardice, but also as a subtle yet sharp critique of the Soviet system. In the scene in question, called "A Cry for Help" (*Krik o pomoshchi*), a man desperately knocks at a row of doors, crying for help. The bureaucrat does not answer; one last cry is heard in the distance before a deathly silence invades the entire space. The doors recall the layers of the frame that surrounds the bureaucrat and emphasize the character's willful isolation from the rest of the world. Their arrangement in perspective, a rare example of three-dimensional space in the film, creates a sense of depth that reflects the deep sin in the conscience of the character. Behind the surface of the character's egoism, a reference to denunciations and arbitrary arrests transpires. Central to the interpretation of this scene is a monument that stands next to the doors, a pillar surmounted by a hand pointing upwards. The hand evokes the character's race to the top ranks, but also strongly recalls an identical hand, and symbol of totalitarian power, as reproduced in a famous animated film created by the Czech director Jiří Trnka in 1965, *The Hand* (*Ruka*), a film that presents a sharp critique of the oppressive communist regime in Czechoslovakia (Figure 1.14).

In this scene, the music and the cries resounding in empty space add to a sense of anguish and oppression. The same oppressive feeling echoes in

FIGURE 1.14 *Man in The Frame.* Scene "A Cry for Help." © Soyuzmultfilm.

the last scene of the film when the bureaucrat climbs to increasingly powerful positions. In this rise, the frame becomes thicker and thicker until it completely engulfs him. The music accompanying his ascension resounds as a parody of an official march turned into circus fanfare, a certain pungent commentary by the composer Boris Shnaper, the force of which might have escaped Khitruk. Nazarov recalls telling Khitruk:

> How wonderfully you dealt with the music! After all, the film is about these idiots and Boris Shnaper distorted 'May Day March!' Fëdor Savel'yevich [Khitruk] turned pale. 'It can't be!'[78]

In the background of this last scene a tower appears with various symbols of everything the character sacrificed in his life for the sake of his career. Passing by these signs of a reality that is foreign to him, not only does the bureaucrat regard them with indifference, but he also appropriates them and degrades them. With his increasing influence, he crosses the borderline of his framed figure and impacts the outside world, he frames and seals the reality that he once consciously rejected and makes it part of his world – flowers get enclosed in frames and butterflies are covered with files and stamps (Figure 1.15).

FIGURE 1.15 *Man in the Frame.* Framing flowers. © Soyuzmultfilm.

His pompous and mechanical hand waving turns him into a grotesque and threatening caricature; his ascent becomes increasingly senseless and dreadful. Once again, Khitruk's criticism reaches from the small world of the character to the larger world of the entire Soviet system, and ultimately becomes a philosophical reflection on human life.

Revised Ending and Official Reception

The film could have ended with the bureaucrat disappearing into the world he created. Instead, the girl skipping rope reappears to provide a positive ending. At the rhythm of the naïve and pure little girl's jumping, the frame that completely enclosed the bureaucrat falls apart (Figure 1.16).

In the original concept, Khitruk did not intend for the film to resolve with the destruction of the bureaucrat by the force of the little girl. During the discussion of the film at the Artistic Council he claims that

> The film was conceived as a biting film; we created it with bite, and we hope that it will help to fight evil. But I would not like to fall back on any epigraph. That would be an unnecessary reassurance.[79]

Originally, the ending depicted how the bureaucrat, lifted by his own frame, reaches "some empty heights, where there was nothing left but this frame."[80] The frame swallows the man and disappears from the empty screen; then, in complete silence and emptiness, a leaflet falls out from the top, the same form from the Employee Personnel Record with the series of "no," with which the

FIGURE 1.16 *Man in the Frame*. Jumping girl and collapsing of the frame. © Soyuzmultfilm.

film started. The hero was born from the record, and at the end of the film, all that remains of him is just the same form, his paper, empty soul.[81] Some members of the Artistic Council considered this end "dangerous, impudent and too sad"[82] and imposed, instead, the reappearance of the girl. This forced ending provided a "more optimistic ring," [83] which certainly conformed to remnants of the official requirements of socialist realism to avoid gloominess in the depiction of reality.

At first, the film was accepted by the Artistic Council, which officially claimed that "On the whole, the film gives the impression of a serious and poignant work, acquiring special interest in the light of the decisions of the 23rd Congress of the CPSU."[84] However, at the end, the film was not shown. The film indeed not only presented a dark picture of the bureaucratic Soviet system portrayed with an unprecedented sharpness, but also offered an image of reality that was far from the socialist realist ideal.[85] As Borodin notices, "Debunking the system of Soviet careerism, the soullessness of its machine, was not the main goal of the authors during the development of the plot," but the film unfolded in a way that "this topic turned out to be the most suitable for showing the evolution of the central image and led to the fact that the film is perceived as a ruthless social diagnosis."[86] The authorities could not accept this criticism. It was 1967, the Thaw euphoria had passed; the film was practically shelved and held back from festivals.[87] Although *Man in the Frame* was not banned officially, it still did not reach a wide public. Khitruk had no choice but to change the ending to have the film released, still he would regret his decision long thereafter.[88]

NOTES

1   Volkov, "Razgovor o professii," 182.
2   Khitruk, *Professiia-animator*, 1: 157.
3   *Fëdor Khitruk. To Be Everything. (Fëdor Khitruk. Byt' Vsem)*.
4   Volkov, "Razgovor o professii," 182.
5   Khrzhanovskii and Khitruk, "Besedy pri iasnoi lune," 84.
6   Zuikov, "Vse reshila sluchainost'," 290. Kurchevskii, "'Rabotat' s Khitrukom trudno...'," 281.
7   Nazarov, "Edik! Est' neplokhaia ideia...," 286. Petrov and Tumelia, "Nauka Udivliat'," 249
8   Kurchevskii, "'Rabotat' s Khitrukom trudno...'," 281; Nazarov, "Edik! Est' neplokhaia ideia...," 283.
9   A more in-depth elaboration of the topic is addressed by the author in the book *Soviet Animation and The Thaw of the 1960s. Not Only for Children.*

10 An attempt in previous years to address topical issues in the short *Emergency Aid* (*Skoraia pomoshch'*, Lamis Bredis, 1948) was not successful. The film was promptly shelved with charges and repercussions on all the artists working on it. Borodin, "Skoraia pomoshch'. Iz istorii mu'tfil'ma Medvedkina," 83.

11 "Satiricheskii kinozhurnal 'Diatel." "Satiricheskii kinozhurnal 'Diatel'." Babichenko, "Dovol'no mul'tshtampov," 37. Borodin, "Animatsiia podnevol'naia," 2005, 114–16.

12 "Govoriat mastera mul'tiplikatsii," 132.

13 Other films were made with puppet animation, such as the film against alcoholism, *The Villain with a Label* (*Zlodeika s nakleikoi*, Stepantsev, Shcherbakov, 1954), and against abuse of power and bureaucratism *The Ballad of the Table* (*Ballada o stole*, Mikhail Kalinin, Roman Davydov, 1955).

14 Mikhailin, "Vysshie formy – 'Za den' do nashei ery' Fedora Khitruka i Iuriia Norsteina."

15 "Smelee iskat' novoe v mul'tiplikatsionnom kino!"; Atamanov, "Protiv naturalizma." Babichenko, "Dovol'no mul'tshtampov."

16 Tsizin, "Fil'my-Skazki"; Atamanov, "Protiv naturalizma"; "Smelee iskat' novoe v mul'tiplikatsionnom kino!" "Govoriat mastera mul'tiplikatsii," 135. The term "naturalism" is particularly charged during Soviet times (see the Campaign against Formalism and Naturalism in 1936), although it has been noted that many elements of the disparaged naturalism can be found in officially praised socialist realist paintings. See discussion on the topic in Silina, "The Struggle Against Naturalism. Soviet Art from the 1920s and 1950s." In discussing Soviet animation, the term is used by the directors as a criticism of those films that have an imitative approach in their depiction of life and merely follow a style based on cliché employed for many years.

17 A more detailed discussion about this important film can be found in Pontieri, *Soviet Animation and the Thaw*, 85–99.

18 *The Spirit of Genius.*

19 Earlier analyses of this film appeared in Pontieri, "Russian Animated Films of the 1960s as a Reflection of the Thaw: Ambiguities and Violation of Boundaries in Story of a Crime."; Pontieri, *Soviet Animation and the Thaw. Not Only for Children.* This chapter shares some comments with the aforementioned publications and refers to concepts previously expanded, but it also provides new insights on certain aspects of the film.

20 Pontieri, Personal Interview with Fëdor Khitruk. Some details also in Khitruk, *Professiia-animator*, 1: 158.

21 Khitruk, *Professiia-animator*, 1: 158. Vol'pin was already famous for the witty dialogues he composed with Nikolai Erdman in many successful live-action films (see for ex. Alexandrov's musicals). Erdman too worked at the studio, a place where many artists and writers would turn to when in conflict with the authorities.

22 Volkov, "Razgovor o professii," 182.

23 *Fëdor Khitruk. Profession Animator*; *Fëdor Khitruk. To Be Everything.* (*Fëdor Khitruk. Byt' Vsem*).

24 Gromov, *S. Alimov: mul'tiplikatsiia, knizhnaia i stankovaia grafika*, 11–2.

25 Gromov, 24.

26 Khitruk, *Professiia-animator*, 1: 159.

27 Khitruk, 1: 159.
28 Khitruk, 1: 160.
29 Maureen Furniss, *Art in Motion. Animation Aesthetic*, 135–53.
30 Khitruk, *Professiia-animator*, 1: 163.
31 Alimov undertook a training session at the Yugoslavian studio in 1966–67. Pontieri, Phone Interview with Sergei Alimov; Pontieri, Personal Interview with Fëdor Khitruk.
32 Halas, *Art in Movement: New Directions in Animation*, 108.
33 Krakauer, *Theory of Film*, 89.
34 Khitruk, *Professiia-animator*, 1: 160.
35 Khitruk, 1: 160.
36 Khitruk, 1: 163.
37 MacFadyen, *Yellow Crocodiles and Blue Oranges*, 144.
38 Eisenstein, "From Lectures on Music and Colour in *Ivan The Terrible*," 184.
39 Pontieri, *Soviet Animation and the Thaw*, 106.
40 Pontieri, 108.
41 Gromov, *S. Alimov: mul'tiplikatsiia, knizhnaia i stankovaia grafika*, 26.
42 Gromov, 26.
43 The fascination for Chaplin dates back to the Soviet avant-garde of the 1920s, see Stepanova's illustrations to the text of Foregger, Kuleshov and Rodchenko in *Kino-Fot*, (3, 1922), or Eisenstein's "Charlie the kid," and Meyerhold's "Chaplin i chaplinizm." It takes form in animation in various ways, including puppet films, such as in the figure of the hunter in *Pencil and Blot* (Evgenii Migunov, 1954).
44 RGALI, "Delo fil'ma *Istoriia odnogo prestupleniia*," 1.
45 The audience does not see a neutral, "unmarked" work, but an adaptation for the screen of Pushkin's *Evgenii Onegin*, a classic that is recognized as part of the Russian collective intellect, another element of the variegated field of *kul'turnost'*. Pontieri, *Soviet Animation and the Thaw*, 115–16.
46 Lotman, "Fenomen kul'tury," 40.
47 Pontieri, *Soviet Animation and the Thaw*, 116.
48 Khitruk, *Professiia-animator*, 1: 164.
49 See the elaboration of the topic individual vs. society in Pontieri, *Soviet Animation and the Thaw*, 112–15.
50 Kelly, *Refining Russia*, 244.
51 Kelly, 251.
52 The discussion of the relevance of *kul'turnost'* in the film as well as the violation of the socialist realist canon is discussed also in Pontieri, *Soviet Animation and the Thaw*, 99–105.
53 Clark, *The Soviet Novel*, 255–60.
54 The most eloquent and original example is the contemporary tale *Fedia Zaitsev*, Valentina and Zinaida Brumberg, 1948), or see for ex. *The Tale of the Old Oak* (*Skazka starogo duba*, Khodataeva, 1949).
55 Pontieri, *Soviet Animation and the Thaw*, 103–4.
56 Part of this subchapter has been discussed in Pontieri, 99–119.
57 I am using the term *concretization* as delineated by Bakhtin in his essay "Forms of Time and the Chronotope," 100.
58 Norstein, "Priznanie masteru," 76.

59 Idleness at work as a target of satire was not new but filled the pages of *Krokodil* as well as made its appearance in a few animated films targeted to an adult public that were release in the late 1950s (see for ex. the film *The Signature is Illegible* (1954).

60 Khitruk, *Professiia-animator*, 1: 160.

61 During the various sessions of the Soyuzmultfilm Artistic Council, the script of *Story of a Crime* went through numerous revisions: the first literary film script for *Story of a Crime* was approved on May 19, 1961, on the condition that some revisions would be made; the second variant was discussed and approved on June 15, 1961, and the directorial film script was discussed and approved a year later, on August 15, 1962. In the protocol of the second session of the Artistic Council for the discussion of *Story of a Crime*'s literary script, an annotation reported the scriptwriter Mikhail Vol'pin's remarks on cutting the script in order to avoid clear references to the poor quality of the *khrushchevki*. RGALI, "Delo fil'ma *Istoriia odnogo prestupleniia*," 122. Pontieri, *Soviet Animation and the Thaw*, 110.

62 RGALI, "Delo fil'ma *Istoriia odnogo prestupleniia*," 123.

63 *The Spirit of Genius*. Quotations as in subtitles. Also qtd. in Pontieri, *Soviet Animation and the Thaw*, 83–4.

64 Khitruk, *Professiia-animator*, 1: 165.

65 Khitruk, 1: 165.

66 Khitruk, 1: 167.

67 An analysis of this film has been published in Pontieri, *Soviet Animation and the Thaw*, 124–39. Some observations are borrowed here and integrated with new insights.

68 Tynianov, "Podporuchik Kizhe"; Khitruk, *Professiia-animator*, 2007, 1: 175.

69 Chekhov, "Chelovek v futliare."

70 Khitruk, *Professiia-animator*, 1: 174.

71 Khitruk, 1: 174.

72 See Alimov's work and the discussion of his style in Gromov, *S. Alimov: mul'tiplikatsiia, knizhnaia i stankovaia grafika.*

73 See the reproductions in Gromov; and Serebrovskii, "Sergei Alimov."

74 Eisenstein, "Za kadrom," 291.

75 It is well known that the category of parasitism could also be stretched to include people unwelcomed by the Soviet authorities. See the trial of Joseph Brodsky in 1964.

76 Khitruk qtd. in Volkov, "Razgovor o professii," 183–84.

77 Khitruk, "From Thought to Image," 27.

78 Nazarov, "Dom na Kaliaevskoi," 42.

79 "Delo Fil'ma 'Chelovek v Ramke'," 20.

80 Khitruk, *Professiia-animator*, 1: 179.

81 Khitruk, 1: 179.

82 Khitruk, 1: 179.

83 "Delo Fil'ma 'Chelovek v Ramke'," 6.

84 Qtd. in Borodin, "Animatsiia podnevol'naia," n.d. ch.5, p.22.

85 Another film released in the same year *The Origin of the Species* (*Proiskhozhdenie vida*, Efim Gamburg, 1966) tackled the theme, instead, with wit and caricature style, comparing the career ascent of an idle worker to the return to the ape stage.

86 Borodin, "Animatsiia podnevol'naia," n.d. Ch. 5, p. 22–3.
87 Maliukova, "Fil'm kak bolevoi refleks," 25.
88 Khitruk, *Professiia-animator*, 1: 179.

Films for Children

2

Toptyzhka (1964), *Bonifatius's Vacation* (1965), and *Vinni Pukh* (1969–72)

INNOVATION OF STYLE IN FILMS FOR CHILDREN

The success with his first directorial film, *Story of a Crime*, prompted Khitruk to explore original styles also in films for children. The six films oriented to a young audience he directed at different times throughout the following decade are some of the most well-known animated films produced in the Soviet Union: *Toptyzhka* (1964), *Bonifatius's Vacation* (*Kanikuli Bonifatsii*, 1965), and the three episodes of Winnie-the-Pooh (*Vinni Pukh*) series. These films are realized in a unique style that accurately reflects each story and its mood. Believing that it is through the form that one can express the content,[1] Khitruk searched for new styles for every film. He detached from the main drawing-on-cel practice and Disney's

DOI: 10.1201/9781003199625-3

typically round traits and smooth movements endorsed in the studio and opted, instead, for a manner characterized by laconic images and sparse yet telling movements and details.

His films for children were popular among spectators of any age; they presented different layers of interpretation that made them appealing to all kinds of audiences. The six shorts mentioned above, though, were made with young people in mind. This was where Khitruk excelled, as he could draw from his many years' experience as animator in children's movies. He himself had an innately youthful spirit, which permeates all his films to the point that people meeting him for the first time never imagined that such a grown-up man could have made them.[2] He put so much into his films that as Zuikov notices, "Khitruk himself is a little of Toptyzhka and a lot of Vinni Pukh."[3]

TOPTYZHKA (1964)

A story of an unlikely friendship between a little hare and a bear cub, born as an assignment in Khitruk's class, became the idea for the film *Toptyzhka*. The simple tale of a cub, who would rather explore the winter surroundings and play with his new friend hare than sleep as every other bear does, is conveyed with such simplicity and lyricism that spectators at any age can relate to the pure joy and carefree excitement enjoyed by the little one playing in the snow. Khitruk regards this film as his best and favorite, "it is the only one of my films in which, when I watch it, I do not squirm from the desire to correct something."[4]

In Pursuit of Charushin's Manner

The inspiration for an aesthetic that could best fit the story came from the drawings of the famous artist and illustrator Evgenii Charushin.[5] Although not a style that could be efficiently adopted in animation, this manner offered an innovative approach for a simple story. As Khitruk argued in defense of the script during the discussion at the studio Artistic Council, "the plot of the story is simple, and the characters are not new. That's why if we did a film with the standard animation devices, it seems to us that it would not be very interesting."[6] The director longed for a return to the rich tradition of Soviet graphic and illustration in animation, "I got stuck in classical animation," he says, "but I knew the animation we had before Soyuzmultfilm, this didn't give me peace, why did we put this wall between animation and graphic culture?"[7]

Drawings on cel with precise and defined outlines, as was the usual practice at the studio, was certainly more easily reproducible for the many drawings needed in the film, but Khitruk felt limited by the traditional style;[8] for this story, he believed that "a hard contour line would ruin the poetics of the tale, would make the images too concrete and as a result the mysterious and enigmatic effect of the Russian folktale would be lost."[9] Charushin's illustrations lack a hard profile, they are realized in color spots and "evanescent strokes,"[10] similar to Chinese watercolor. They convey a tangible sense of fluffiness and softness in the characters' fur as though their images were not confined to the paper.

Transposing this effect on animation was arduous work. Years earlier, Khitruk worked as animator on a film, *The Disobedient Kitten* (*Neposlushnyi kotenok*, Pashchenko, 1953), which first strived to convey the fluffiness of the texture of animal fur. This film, simple in its message and story, as in the tradition of films for younger children flourishing at Soyuzmultfilm, avoided the harsh contour typical of the drawings on celluloid sheet by means of double exposure and the use of masks.[11] With *Toptyzhka*, instead, Khitruk aimed to achieve a contour-less effect through strokes and drawings. Charushin's drawing style, which always fascinated him, seemed to fit perfectly the purpose.[12]

The texture of these drawings is particularly attractive for the very young audience, as it provides a visual texture that appeals to young children in their discovery of the world through touch. Also, as the animation scholar Krivulia argues, "the feeling of fluffiness and softness of the images of the bear cub and the little hare creates a sense of deep empathy, closeness to the heroes of the film, who are captivating with their naïveté and childish innocence"[13] (Figure 2.1).

As in other films made by Khitruk and the art director Sergei Alimov, the drawings have only a few details but are chosen in a way to reveal the essential characteristics of the figures and environment and trigger the desired effect on the spectator. The audience could almost feel not only the softness of Toptyzhka's fur, but also the coziness of the interior of his house, as well as the crispness and enchantment of the winter landscape.

At first, the team tried a new method of drawing, not with pencil and ink, but with foam rubber sponges used as stamps, by tapping on the top of the drawn image.[14] This technique, however, was not very efficient, and the artist Nosyrev offered to create flat marionettes, i.e., cut-out with hinge joints,[15] which allowed the figures to maintain their soft profile and richness in texture in various phases (Figure 2.2).

Flat marionettes have an additional advantage; they can pause in stillness. An animated drawing, once frozen, reveals the inert form that is at its basis; in full animation (not so much in limited animation where the effect fits the overall conventionality of the style) a frozen image risks becoming lifeless. Flat marionettes, instead, create their own conventionality, a static

FIGURE 2.1 *Toptyzhka*. Toptyzhka and the hare. Cel. © Soyuzmultfilm.

FIGURE 2.2 *Toptyzhka*. Flat marionette. © Soyuzmultfilm.

pause reveals the essence of the original work of art. In this film, the flat marionette enlivens the texture and the almost tangible sensation of fur in the drawings; even if the marionette comes to a still, it is as alive as a plush toy in a child's hand.

Animal Sounds, Narrator Voice, and Music

The young spectators are called to give a voice to the characters just as in their games. The animals in the film are anthropomorphized, but they are not gifted with a human voice, as in the traditional animated films for children Khitruk worked on until then. The characters here talk with their own sound, in a conventional bear and hare language, expressing the meaning of their talk with gestures and intonation. Their voices make the young audience realize the characters belong to the animal world even if they sleep, walk, and play as little children which, in a child's playful mind, is a perfectly acceptable alternative reality.

The narrator recounts the story and translates the characters' sounds into human words. The narrative commentary, which has all the warmth and inflection of a grandmother's voice, brings the audience back to traditional storytelling and the realm of folktales. The world so created is filled with folkloric details, from the bear sleeping on the top of the wooden stove, to details in the décor, such as the quilt blankets and the window decoration[16] (Figure 2.3).

Also the organization of the frame evokes the illustrations from folktales. The best example of this appears in the last scene when a picture of the characters sitting around a samovar, drinking their tea from a little plate, is framed by branches of red viburnum (Figure 2.4).

In addition to the animals' noises and narrator's voice, music provides another layer of sound; it accompanies the characters' growls and enhances their musicality as well as the tone of the conversations. At times, music marks the narrator's warm voice and emphasizes the overall lyrical and sentimental atmosphere of the film; at other times, it underscores a contrapuntal play of sound and image that reveals a subtle humor. The playful music often revives conventions of the circus. The composer Mieczysław (Moisei) Weinberg, indeed, wrote several scores for circus performances (more about him in *Boniface's Vacation* and *Vinni Pukh*). From the very beginning, the music accompanies the title in an upbeat melody with xylophones and flutes reminiscent of a circus setting; then, throughout the film, the music marks the mute performance of the characters, as it would underline a clown gesture. The scene when the outraged mother dismisses Toptyzhka's desire to go out and play in the snow provides an example of how music offers a second layer of a gesture: the mother finishes her rebut, turns her back and covers herself with the blanket; her feet stick out, they rub together and then, finally, come to a still at the sound of a trombone note

FIGURE 2.3 *Toptyzhka*. Inside the izba folkloric elements. © Soyuzmultfilm.

FIGURE 2.4 *Toptyzhka*. Tea Party. Organization of the frame. © Soyuzmultfilm.

with the closing effect of a full stop.[17] Music in all its manifestation becomes an essential element of this film. It is, according to Khitruk, "the breath of the film"[18] that then materializes in images and movements.

Inner World behind Images and Movements

The little cub's mind transpires through associations of images, what Silant'eva calls a "pictorial plot." As Toptyzhka first ventures in the woods, the image of a red sun that turns into the crimson belly of a bird exemplifies in a simple image the inner journey of the main character, from aiming for something as distant and unknown as the sun, to something concrete and known, in the present bird.[19]

The character's inner world breaks through also in essential gestures, given sparsely but with precise details. A simple image of Toptyzhka's feet still in motion while his eyes fix on a beautiful flower reveals the child's conflictual desire to run freely and explore the world and, at the same time, his need to keep his mother in sight and follow the rules.[20]

As already noted, in his work as animator, Khitruk is a master at finding a dominant gesture that would give meaning to the entire scene. The gesture can unveil a character feature, a psychological trait, and an emotional factor; there is no better image than a little paw cleaning the window enough to peek out to expose Toptyzhka's longing for his friend (Figure 2.5).

The window in itself is a motif in the film that acquires multiple functions, spatial, temporal, psychological and dramaturgic: the window creates a physical barrier between the characters, the view from the window shows the changing of the seasons, then a layer of obstacles "melts" with its thaw. It is also a physical barrier that encircles the narrowmindedness voiced by the mother bear: "Have you ever seen bears roam the forest in winter? Sleep!" "Have you ever seen bears and hares be friends?" The mother asserts her blind acceptance of a status quo that only an innocent and naïve child's courageous act can challenge. The morale fostering open-mindedness and conciliatory power is not only dear to Khitruk, but it is also self-referential considering the steps undertaken by Khitruk to challenge the dominant style in the studio. Ultimately, the depiction of a child's discovery of the world with such naïveté, curiosity and simplicity offers a truthful picture of the children's world that goes beyond moralizing.

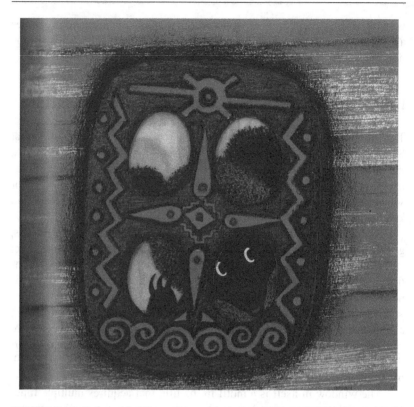

FIGURE 2.5   *Toptyzhka*. Toptyzhka at the window. © Soyuzmultfilm.

BONIFATIUS'S VACATION (1965)

After *Toptyzhka*, Khitruk embarked on a second film for children, *Bonifatius's Vacation* (1965). The film is based on a fable by the Czech writer Miloš Macourek,[21] "Bonifatius's and his family" ("Bonifác a bratránci") readapted for the screen by Khitruk himself.

The story of a circus lion who goes to visit his beloved grandmother and ends up performing for the local children for the entire vacation sparked the director's attention. The morale of the film – the joy of sharing one own's creation, the destiny of the artist to be always on the job, and the cherished relationship with the public – strongly resonated with Khitruk's personality. Khitruk himself admitted the film was quite autobiographical.[22]

When planning the film, the director divided the subject into separate episodes, each of a specific length to maintain the desired rhythm. Every episode was based on a singular "attraction" and developed according to what he calls "lines of mood," i.e., details about the mood of the characters as well as speculations about the audience's corresponding reaction.[23] The term "attraction," just as in Eisenstein's well-known article,[24] underlines the impact of a device on the spectator.[25] But it was not the highly ideological premises of Eisenstein's thought that fascinated Khitruk, rather the common intention to affect the audience. While Khitruk was greatly influenced by Eisenstein's theories on film structure, frame composition, rhythm, color, and montage, he carefully edited his films, not with the intention to hit or shock the spectators as in Eisenstein's early works, but rather to enchant them with a rhythmic montage made of carefully timed shots and a contrapuntal composition of images and sound.

A Charming Character and Fragmented Bodies

From the very beginning, the character of Bonifatius enthralls the audience with his slightly grotesque look and reserved disposition. His gentle and benevolent manners perfectly suit his elegant bearing topped with an oversized head and bushy mane, which gives him a slightly comic but friendly demeanor. The entire movie revolves around him; the absence of conflict between a protagonist and antagonists creates a story made of moods that range from lyricism to laughter. While making the film, Khitruk recalls, "I hoped that the film would be within the mental grasp of any age, [...] the artist Sergei Alimov and I chose a grotesque style of drawing to make our heroes look both funny and touching."[26]

From his very first appearance, Bonifatius contradicts the expected image of a ferocious beast. The circus advertising poster featuring a wide-open, scary, roaring mouth fills the entire frame; but soon after, the camera pans back from this image to show a pensive Bonifatius, rather nervous of the public, sitting with his head resting on his hand. "All his appearance," the original film script says,

> posture, and facial expressions are the complete opposite of what is depicted on the poster. Nothing ferocious or regal – just a tired and lonely lion, who modestly sits in the corner on a bench and pensively eats a banana[27] (Figure 2.6).

His power relies more on his ability to entertain than his manifestation of physical strength; his threatening roar is an acting gesture, unmasked only by the perceptive children of the island. A parody of his presumed strength

FIGURE 2.6   *Bonifatius*. Circus poster. Cel. © Soyuzmultfilm.

reaches the peak with the imitation of the strongman lifting weights. The oversized torso in this scene balances on his short legs as his huge head and mane stay put in a precarious equilibrium (Figure 2.7).

His head became the hardest challenge for the animators:

> Bonifatius proved to be incredibly difficult to work with. It could not be rotated; it could not be drawn in front. The charm would be gone. How we tormented ourselves! But he looked good in profile, and we tried to keep the magic of his profile.[28]

His beautiful mane, a cut-out with soft contour apposed to the drawings,[29] recalls the softness achieved in *Toptyzhka*, and, as in the previous film, it has a peculiar charm.

FIGURE 2.7 *Bonifatius.* Strongman number. © Soyuzmultfilm.

Not only Bonifatius but also other characters are realized in cut-outs, especially in the circus scenes. The circus director is realized as a flat marionette (Figure 2.8), and so are the performers, for whom Khitruk seems to have drawn inspiration from Trnka's film *The Merry Circus* (*Veselý Cirkus*, 1951).

In both films, the circus setting is stylized, while cut-outs and flat marionettes convey a mechanical quality to the performers' gestures. The performances are so turned into highly conventionalized games, in which the audience takes part in contrapuntal montage in the form of discrete units, modernistic fragmented images, collages of many faces or disjointed hands, and fragmented body parts (Figure 2.9).

The conventionality of the cut-outs is maximally expressed in the clown number, which inevitably recalls the beginning of *Ballet mécanique* (Fernand Léger, 1924) in which a cubist rendition of Charlie Chaplin is formed with disjointed parts that detach and reassemble at the author's caprice, as in a cubist picture. In Khitruk's film too the clowns are disjointed marionettes reduced to geometrical fragments that collapse and rearrange at the whims of slapstick gags (Figure 2.10).

FIGURE 2.8 *Bonifatius*. Director marionette. © Soyuzmultfilm.

FIGURE 2.9 *Bonifatius*. Disembodied faces and hands. © Soyuzmultfilm.

FIGURE 2.10 *Bonifatius*. Clown scene. © Soyuzmultfilm.

Mechanization of the body and fascination with clownery bring the film back to the tradition of the Soviet avant-garde of the 1920s and 1930s – it is enough to think of Meyerhold's stagings, a mixture of scientific biomechanics and circus feats[30]. Besides, specific details of circus life reference classical Soviet musicals. The backstage scenes with dancers passing by kissing Bonifatius, the bicycles from the beginning of the century, the strongman's inflated muscles, the men carrying the fence to build the lion cage, the comic juxtaposition of posters with fictional reality, all these details vividly recall Grigorii Alexandrov's musical *The Circus* (1936) and its humorous expedients.

Musical Commentaries

The world of the circus is realized in Khitruk's film from the very first frame. The credits appear with fonts reminiscent of circus posters. The music in the background, apparently non-diegetic, punctuates each shifting credit board with clangs of cymbals. Only when the credit scrolls reach the end is the music revealed to be diegetic and cymbals and trumpets materialize on the screen.

From the beginning, Khitruk creates a polyphony of sounds, image, and movement that creates an "allegretto" rhythm, which properly suits the circus mood. The composer, Mieczysław Weinberg, picked up from this mood to elaborate the most suitable music. Weinberg could easily attune to Khitruk's intention and collaborated with him on several films, from *Toptyzhka* to the series dedicated to Winnie the Pooh and his last film *The Lion and the Bull*. His repertoire ranged from numerous string-quartets, symphonies, and sonatas to soundtracks for animated films, as well as live-action movies (the most internationally famous probably being *The Cranes are Flying*).[31] Weinberg also wrote scores for ballet, theater performances, and a large collection of circus music.[32] His sensibility toward circus music certainly suited the theme and the images of *Bonifatius's Vacation*, and helped to create a contrapuntal effect of sound and image that was so important in Khitruk's film. The music alternates accents and contrasts, instrumentation and pauses, to form a varied rhythm that keeps the audience engaged. Often the music becomes fragmented and fulfills a dramaturgic role; a few notes may accompany a gesture, then a string of notes or an effective staccato respond, forming lines of a wordless dialogue between the characters. These notes, the narrative voice, as well as images and gestures, create a complex polyphony that only a master of rhythm like Khitruk could design in his mind.[33] A vacation theme recurs in the film to mark each episode; first, it takes the form of a song heard from a traveling school bus; then, it echoes in the moment Bonifatius sets off for his grandmother's house; and ultimately, repeats every time Bonifatius heads for the lake, dreaming of catching a magical goldfish. Each time his attempts are frustrated by the interruptions of the children asking to be entertained, until the intervals between the refrains become increasingly short and then completely disappear. The music becomes a continuous soundtrack of the entire vacation spent performing for the young inhabitants of the island.

The music also supports Bonifatius's performances and in general underlines, with its fanfares and bravura marches, the obvious theme of the circus. Elaborated with original variations, the music at times betrays the influence of Weinberg's close friend and colleague, Shostakovich.[34] Most importantly, the soundtrack helps to complement the depiction of Bonifatius's character. The music accompanies him during his circus numbers, from the frightening performance with the tamer, to the suspenseful acrobatics on a tightrope, to the multiple tricks and roles he plays for the children on the island. It reveals with its variations how Bonifatius embodies in himself the joy, fun, and lightness, in a word, the quintessence of the circus, but it also subtly unveils through chosen melodic chords his more intimate character, his caring and easygoing demeanor, at ease whenever he does not need to put on a frightening mask foreign to him. Bonifatius's kind disposition transpires throughout the film in many ways, but music is certainly one of the fundamental factors in creating a lyrical atmosphere.

Conventionalized Style

In the film, details and movements are reduced to a minimum, while spatial and time relations are highly conventionalized. By offering a conventionalized style, the director played on the spectators' ability to fill in the gaps with their imagination or to rely on a subconscious mechanism that would accept the convention. The trip to Africa takes no time on miniature trains and boats, and movements are distilled in key poses (Figure 2.11).

The circus performers' movements are reduced to the essential so as to underline that Bergsonian mechanical aura that triggers laughter.[35] The entire film develops under the motto of maximum expressiveness through minimal and essential means that Khitruk adopted from his very first film. But, it is not only movements that are reduced to a minimum; in this film, Khitruk reaches the extreme by reducing the entire screen to a black frame for about six seconds while Bonifatius travels by train under a tunnel. As Mikhailin notices, the blackness of the screen is not perceived as an interruption of the

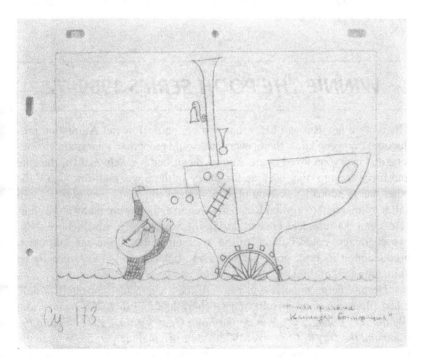

FIGURE 2.11 *Bonifatius*. On the boat. Key drawing. © Soyuzmultfilm.

action, rather it is filled in by the audience's ability to complete the picture.[36] The spectator becomes co-author of the film.

On the other hand, the audience in the story appears to have a marginal position. The spectators at the circus appear as a conglomerate of bodyless faces and hands, and the children on the island all look alike, are delineated in simple traits, and move en masse. The audience is there to perform a function, not to depict a character. Nonetheless, in this pseudo-self-referential film, the spectators' function is not less important. For Khitruk, being at the service of the audience is the artist's destiny and call; it is an inner desire that brings happiness and, want it or not, overcomes any other wish that a magical goldfish could grant. The realization that the path to happiness is ultimately within oneself takes the form of the elusive goldfish caught inside Bonifatius's sweater. Only now does Bonifatius realize that he does not need magic to be happy and so willingly sets the wish-granting fish free.

Bonifatius's Vacation is a film of bright colors and mood, enthralling all children and nostalgic adults alike. Accurately thought-of details during the production of the film, from the script stage to completion, shape a film which is entertaining and lyrical at the same time; a film with that ungraspable quality that makes a work of art.

WINNIE THE POOH SERIES 1969–72

There are a few Russian films that best epitomized Soviet Animation production; everyone knew them, everyone would recognize their main characters, and everyone loved them. Among them, one is *Cheburashka*, the cute and furry creature that became the image in the Soyuzmultfilm logo,[37] the other one is Khitruk's version of Winnie the Pooh, or *Vinni Pukh* as I will call it following the original Russian. Of course, there were many more characters and masterpieces created during the Soviet years, but I believe these two characters could be singled out to be emblems of Russian animation production at its best: good hearted, philosophical, and kindly moralizing animation for children.

Despite being popular and beloved, these characters appeared in only a few films, just four episodes for Cheburashka and three for Vinni Pukh (*Winnie the Pooh*, 1969; *Winnie the Pooh Goes Visiting*, 1971; *Winnie the Pooh and the Day of Concerns*, 1972).[38] The original idea for the Winnie the Pooh series was to film nine episodes, but the project did not go beyond the third, "we did the first – it was good, I liked it," says Khitruk, "The second one was worse; at the third one I felt that I could not do it anymore. I'm not able to do a serial stream, even if it meant getting rich."[39]

A series presents some advantages. The first film of the series is like a "pilot," a test of the system of images of the entire series in which "the type, the character, the kind of relationships and the line of behavior of each character are built up."[40] Once this is established, the second film does not need a thorough introduction, because the director assumes that the spectator is already familiar with the characters and the general situation.[41] Flaws of the "pilot" first episode can be checked and fixed, but in general more time can be dedicated to conceive comedic situations and funny tricks. Some directors, though, see in that initial search the most important aspect of a new film, and feel that once they have it, the interest in the film diminishes; as Volkov points out, Khitruk is one of them.[42]

To a Western public, the name of Winnie the Pooh is associated with Disney's film, often even forgetting that Disney was not the original creator of the character. Khitruk, instead, was not aware of Disney's film; he had the occasion to watch the film only in 1975, when he visited the Walt Disney studio[43] and had a chance to meet Wolfgang Reitherman, the director of the first two shorts on Winnie released by Disney, *Winnie the Pooh and the Honey Tree* (1966) and *Winnie the Pooh and the Blustery day* (1968).[44] With hindsight, Khitruk did not particularly like Disney's version,[45] but was proud of recalling how Reitherman, once he saw his movie, declared that the Soviet version was more successful.[46] The film became a symbol of national pride.

Both the American and Russian Winnie the Pooh were adaptations from the famous A. A. Milne's story published first in 1926; but, while the American adaptation was quite faithful to the text, Khitruk's film offered some major variations. The *Vinni Pukh* series is based on the translation of A. A. Milne's story by Boris Zakhoder,[47] which Khitruk recognized and gave credit for.[48] However, Khitruk elaborated his own variation. He was acquainted with the original English version[49] and wrote the literary script with the film already in mind; thus, strictly speaking, it was not a typical literary script.[50]

The main discrepancy between Milne's story (as well as the rendition on the screen by Reitherman) and Khitruk's script is the absence of Christopher Robin. In Khitruk's film, Christopher Robin's cues were redistributed among Pooh's friends, who are not the boy's toys as in the original story, but rather they live in their own reality. "For us," says Khitruk, "there was only one world – the world of Vinni Pukh. They are not animals or people – they are characters."[51] The story development of this film went relatively effortlessly, Khitruk says; the search for the stylist choices, instead, was less smooth.[52]

In Search of Unique Stylistic Choices

While Disney's film based its stylistic choices on the original illustrations of Ernest H. Shepard, Khitruk wanted to depart from this style and look for original solutions. E.H. Shepard illustrated some of the animal characters, such as the rabbit and the owl, in a realistic way, but others, namely Winnie the Pooh, Piglet, and Eeyore, were drawn from toys. In the Disney's film, Reitherman faithfully followed Shepard's drawing of Winnie, Piglet, Eeyore, Kanga, and Roo (these last two are not present in Khitruk's films), but he gave the rabbit and the owl more cartoonish features. The Hundred Acre Wood was depicted in a naturalistic way in the original illustrations as well as in the film.

Khitruk's art directors, Vladimir Zuikov, assisted by Eduard Nazarov, instead, looked for original traits in the characters and opted for a more conventionalized representation of the environment, reminiscent of children's drawings. The idea of adopting a childlike manner might have sprung from the map that opens Milne's book. A drawn map of the forest, filled with misspelled words, is completed with a caption that cites "Drawn by me and Mr. Shepard helpd [sic]." Khitruk's film, similarly, begins with a map, but there is no mention of Christopher Robin's authorship. The names of various locations appear in the form of repetitions and alliterations worthy of Vinni's poetic disposition (Figure 2.12).

FIGURE 2.12 *Vinni Pukh*. Map. Sketch. © Soyuzmultfilm.

The style recalls children's drawings with a stylized depiction of trees and flowers, and profiles with two eyes (Figure 2.13).

Multiple colored crayon strokes and the absence of sharp contours provide the grass and trees with texture and an almost tactile experience. The characters, although developed and colored on traditional cels, have an irregular and mobile contour that harmonizes with the background. The result is an imaginative world, filled with children's play conventions, in which there is no space for human figures or naturalistic representation of the environment as in Disney's version.

Khitruk's team worked hard to find a look for Vinni that would convey the simple but at the same time philosophical and poetic character of the protagonist. In addition, they had to consider a figure whose traits and movements would be easily reproducible.[53] In an interview conducted several years after the film, Zuikov still remembered the challenge to subdue to the idea that the studio was a factory with strict deadlines, which would not allow freedom to draw unusual characters or employing artistic techniques that would not easily turn into animation. Khitruk, at home with the studio's policies, constantly worked with the world of animation in mind, considering what could be efficiently elaborated by the studio artists in the time at their disposal. Khitruk was always open to artists' ideas – although sometimes, as

FIGURE 2.13 *Vinni Pukh.* Conventionalized children's drawings. Sketch of background. © Soyuzmultfilm.

Zuikov puts it, he needed some convincing arguments[54] – for him, the creation of the film was a collective work,[55]

> I have always used the images that artists and art directors created for me
> – Sergei Alimov, Vladimir Zuikov and others. They drew much better than
> me, they had richer imagination and graphic style and more professional
> experience. But it was me who gave them the direction of their search – I
> offered a kind of verbal portrait of the hero. For example, Volodia Zuikov
> found Piatachok from the very first sketch, but we searched for Winnie the
> Pooh for quite a long time.[56]

To find the right visual choice for the protagonist was a daunting task among
hundreds of bears in animation. The first prototype for Vinni was a teddy
bear (Zuikov's) which could not turn his head.[57] Many variations followed,
until Nazarov elaborated the final figure: a round, rather squat shaped, chubby
cub, whose head with a crumpled ear (such because he sleeps on it, Khitruk
would say)[58] is devoid of a neck. His round body stoutly connected to the head
moves in unison with the rest of the body and makes every turn a feat, a challenge that is better explained by Eduard Nazarov,

> That means, he must bow with all the body, turn with all the body, look up
> with all the body. He cannot turn his head strongly, only a little. And so,
> since our Vinni Pukh is all about impossibilities, then try to do something
> with him! But here is where the interest arises. You start to look for impossible physical positions. Do you remember how Vinni Pukh looked into
> the hole? He entirely rolled over, the bottom took the place of the head;
> and it was still necessary to find the balance of this whole nightmare. A
> normal character couldn't have this position. How much paper I used up
> with drawings![59]

Vinni's big eyes reveal an array of expressions from pensive meditation and
creative pondering to child-like awe. His furry texture is conveyed with an
irregular thick contour. Originally, he was all furry, but in order not to have
to draw all the hairs for thousands of drawings, they decided to shave him![60]
Other peculiar traits are his absent arms substituted by big paws with long,
internally rotated claws, and legs detached from the body (Figure 2.14).

His bearing perfectly suits his character, his arms move together (and
not synchronized arm and opposite leg). His peculiar gait was the fruit of a
mistake that Khitruk meant to correct, but Zuikov and others thought that
was precisely the right gait for the character.[61] The funny way in which the
hero moves perfectly fits his round body and emphasizes his pensive and
naïve personality.

While Vinni is a poet, a dreamer, and in a way a philosopher, the little
pig Piatachok (Piglet) is his disciple, a faithful audience for Vinni's poetic
creation (Figure 2.15).

FIGURE 2.14 *Vinni Pukh*. Vinni. © Soyuzmultfilm.

FIGURE 2.15 *Vinni Pukh*. Vinni Pukh and Piatachok. Key frames. © Soyuzmultfilm.

His miniature size, accentuated by his thin neck (a successful and cute detail in comparison with Disney's stouter version) and his light gait ever "two centimeters above the ground,"[62] suits his position constantly a few steps behind Vinni physically and mentally; he stumbles against Vinni every time his friend suddenly stops, and he always understands what Vinni says a few seconds late. His interactions with Vinni contribute to the humorous and witty tone of the film and serve on a pure sound and rhythmical level.

Although the pair Vinni–Piatachok is driving the narrative, other characters appear in the following episodes. In the second film we meet Krolik (Rabbit), a tall and slim figure, with small feet, spectacles and protruding front teeth which give him an intellectual look that suits his polite and proper behavior (Figure 2.16).

Only in the third episode, the longest (20-minutes long instead of ten), do we meet other characters: the donkey Ia, which is very similar to Disney's Eeyore, apart from being brown in color instead of blue, and Sava (the owl) a short and chubbier version of Disney's Owl in his *Winnie the Pooh*, yet a close, although simplified, rendition of the owl in *Bambi* (Figures 2.17 and 2.18).

Each one of them has a distinct personality and a peculiar way of speaking, which marks the rhythm of the exchanges and provides the tone of the scene.

FIGURE 2.16   *Vinni Pukh*. Krolik. © Soyuzmultfilm.

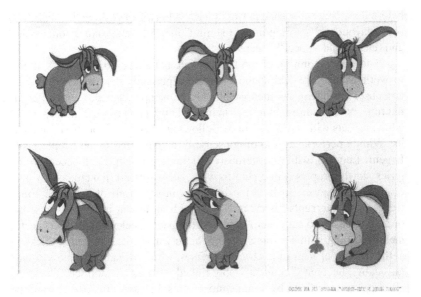

FIGURE 2.17 *Vinni Pukh*. Ia the donkey. © Soyuzmultfilm.

FIGURE 2.18 *Vinni Pukh*. Sava the owl. © Soyuzmultfilm.

Sound, Music, and Voice

Sound is inextricably linked with images in all Khitruk's films, but in this series, the director reached the highest point of his mastery. Khitruk identified all fundamental accents, every change in rhythm, in tone or action even before the composer started to work on it.[63] Khitruk talks about the music and sound layout as a "cardiogram of the film;" in it, all changes of mood, tension and release find a specific beat.[64]

The very beginning of the first episode is the apex of Khitruk's ability to work with image and sound to create a perfectly detailed rhythm. The composer Weinberg sets the tone already in the opening titles with an original tune, a "meandering nursery-rhyme-style tune played on Harpsichord,"[65] which repeats with variations in the following episodes. Soon after the credits, Winnie performs a solo of nonsense lyric (delivered by an irreplaceable Evgenii Leonov), while boisterously striding on a path. Each accent in the lyrics slowly propels him a step forward; all words are punctuated by precisely timed pauses, such as the instances in which all of a sudden Vinni freezes and interrupts his creative flow with an urgent need to express his insatiable desire to eat. Then, suddenly, the pace accelerates, and a cheerful melody, a song with a "'sprechgesang' quality about its notation,"[66] kicks in at the rhythm of Vinni's poetry. The verses, which already have an intrinsic musicality, become thus inextricably linked with the soundtrack. The overall effect is underlined by Vinni's movements, his steps, his pauses, and the unexpected explosion of monosyllabic words followed by some equally unexpected movement of extraneous elements, such as jumping fish!

In the second film, the music becomes even more complex as it follows the two lines of Vinni Pukh and Piatachok. A music with cabaret undertones tailgates the declamation of the verses, which is interrupted by scraps of dialogue between Piatachok and Vinni. If Piatachok parrots Vinni by repeating with a delay his last two words, the symphonic music presents a similar composition; the fanfare that accompanies Vinni Pukh follows a higher-pitched string phrase that fits Piatachok's squeaky voice. Not only does the cadence of the verses provide the musicality and rhythm, one of the highest achievements for this film, but it also suggests a light parody of poetical writing typical of the early Revolutionary years; just think of Mayakovsky's stride along the streets to find the rhythm for his bombastic poems.[67] The declamatory tone remains incomplete, Vinni is still at a stage of word searching; as Alexander Prokhorov notices, Khitruk avoids the "monologic didacticism" typical of early Soviet animation and opts instead for double-voiced, ironic discourse.[68] Irony is achieved with the juxtaposition of Vinni's seriousness in composing poetry and simple, hilarious, pun-filled lyrics as a result. An added humorous tone is triggered by Piatachok stumbling over Vinni at every one of his turns or sudden stops.

With each of Piatachok's stumbles, the spectators re-orient themselves; it is a "game with the spectator, says Khitruk."[69] In order for this "game" to be effective, Khitruk carefully worked on every small detail that would assure the audience's adequate reaction.[70] The overall witty effect is underlined by Evgenii Leonov's acting and sped up voice, which gives Vinni's voice a higher pitch,[71] juxtaposed with Iia Savvina's imitation of Bella Akhmadulina's voice for her Piatachok, a choice that contributed to the parodic effect.[72]

Also the narrator serves the ironic discourse by presenting puns with a deadpan intonation that makes the plays on words already present in the text even more hilarious. At the same time, the actor Vladimir Osenev's warm narrator voice conveys the overall simple, benign, humorous atmosphere present in the book. Vinni is a poet, but in a simple, dreamy way; his poetry and philosophizing is grounded, based on everyday life needs, vices, and friendly acts. Ironic philosophy reigns in the film and appeals to every age; the humor is not for slapstick's sake, as "the film touches some strings of the human soul."[73]

Vinni Pukh is the only character that Khitruk gifts with a voice. All of Khitruk's other films are without dialogue, most of them have only a narrative voice. Perhaps because of this or because of the complexity of such a simple character, the search for the perfect actor in this role was particularly difficult. It took some effort to convince Leonov to accept the role, but once he accepted, Khitruk recalls, "he immediately and accurately caught the character of the hero."[74] Incidentally, with Erast Garin, another Soviet star in the cast, the dubbing did not go as smoothly.[75]

Vinni Pukh has lots in common with Khitruk, or perhaps vice versa. Nazarov noticed how certain gestures are typical of Khitruk's, like his way of turning with the entire body.[76] Maliukova also notices, "Winnie himself, with his concentration, stubbornness, and desire to get to the bottom of the truth, suspiciously resembles Fëdor Savel'evich."[77] Indeed, Khitruk and Vinni have many character traits in common; their pauses while in serious concentration, their search for the right rhythm, their keenness to enjoy the world surrounding them, their determination, and endless imagination.

NOTES

1 Khitruk, *Professiia-animator*, 2007, 2: 113.
2 Petrov and Tumelia, "Nauka udivliat'," 257. Aldashin, "O Khitruke," 275.
3 Zuikov, "Vse reshila sluchainost'," 286.
4 Khitruk, *Professiia-animator*, 2007, 1: 171.
5 Khitruk, 1: 168.
6 "Toptyzhka. Protokol Zasedeniia Khudozhestvennogo Soveta Ot 14.6.63," 1.
7 Khitruk, *Professiia-animator*, 2007, 2: 113.
8 Khitruk, 2: 113.
9 Volkov, "Razgovor o professii," 183.
10 Khitruk, *Professiia-animator*, 2007, 2: 113.

11 Ivanov-Vano, *Kadr za kadrom*, 135. Another later film for young children, *Four From a Backyard* (*Chetvero s odnogo Dvora*, Inessa Kovalevskaia, 1967), utilizes instead a mixture of drawings and flat marionettes that recalls *Toptyzhka*'s style. However, their stylization is brought to the extreme and, although the drawings aim to reproduce the soft texture of the animal characters, the film lacks the warmth and lyricism present in Khitruk's film. More successful in conveying a poetic vein were films made with puppets: *Who Said Miaow* (*Kto skazal miau*, Vladimir Degtiarev, 1962) employs puppets and a simple plot to present a similar journey in search of truth; later, Kachanov's *Varezhka* (1967) and Kurchevskii's *Frantishek* (1967) will address young children with lyrical puppet films.

12 Maliukova, "Poteriav, ne chuvstvoval sebia poteriannym."

13 Krivulia, *Labirinty animatsii*, 62.

14 Khitruk, *Professiia-animator*, 2007, 2: 113.

15 Khitruk, 2: 113.

16 Other films of these years follow a new tendency to return to folklore seeking a "national" character in Russian animation. A good example of this tendency is *The Left-Handed Craftsman* (*Levsha*, Ivan Ivanov-Vano, 1964), made in the same year as *Toptyzhka* and based on engravings and *lubok* style. Also Leonid Nosyrev, who worked with Khitruk in *Toptyzhka*, will continue the tradition of folkloric elements in several films made in the 1970s and 1980s, among the most famous, *If You Don't Like It, Do Not Listen* (*Ne liubo - ne slushai*, 1977), *Rain* (*Dozhd'*, 1978), *The Magical Ring* (*Volshebnoe kol'tso*, 1979), and *Arkhangelsk Stories* (*Arkhangel'skie novelly*, 1986). It is also worth noting how Eisenstein, despite his respect for Disney, had repeatedly raised the question of the use of folk-art motifs in animated films instead of blindly imitating Disney's style. Eisenstein, "Viatskaia loshadka."

17 *Toptyzhka*, 1'31."

18 Khitruk once commented how listening to the prerecording sound for the film, he closed his eyes and he could hear the breath of this film. *Fëdor Khitruk. Profession Animator.*

19 Silant'eva, "Sedmoe iskusstvo," 16.

20 *Toptyzhka*, 7'04."

21 The Czech writer also wrote the story which formed the basis of another very famous film of the 1960s, *Frantishek* (Vadim Kurchevskii, 1967).

22 Khitruk, *Professiia-animator*, 2007, 1: 171.

23 This was a technique that Khitruk learned from Mstislav Pashchenko, who would not only make notes of the mood of the characters in the director script, but he would also plan in advance which kind of reaction these feelings could provoke in the spectator. Khitruk, 1: 172.

24 Eisenstein, "The Montage of Attractions," 30; Eisenstein, "The Montage of Film Attractions," 35–6.

25 Khitruk, *Professiia-animator*, 2007, 1: 172.

26 Khitruk, "From Thought to Image," 27.

27 "'Kanikuly Bonifatsiia' Stsenarii mul'tiplikatsionnogo fil'ma F. Khitruka. Po skazke cheshkogo pisatelia Milana Matsoureka 'Bonifatsii i ego rodstvenniki' - 2 Chasti."

28 Maliukova, "Poteriav, ne chuvstvoval sebia poteriannym." Maliukova, "Fil'm kak bolevoi refleks," 25.

29 Khitruk, *Professiia-animator*, 2007, 2: 113.
30 Circus appeal was not only a Russian cinema phenomenon, see Charlie Chaplin's film *The Circus* (1928), as well as his acting style, or later Disney's film *Dumbo* (1941) also based on Circus life.
31 Music-Weinberg, "Mieczysław Weinberg. The Composer and His Music."
32 Elphick, "Lines That Have Escaped Destruction. Researching the Life and Music of Mieczysław Weinberg." More about the composer can be found in Mogl, *Juden, die ins Lied sich retten - der Komponist Mieczyslaw Weinberg (1919–1996) in der Sowjetunion.*
33 See Norstein about Khitruk in Norstein, "On vnes inoe ponimanie izobrazheniia...," 244–45.
34 Elphick noticed how this influence is perceived especially in the clown scene. Elphick, "Cartoon Time."
35 Bergson, *Laughter : An Essay on the Meaning of the Comic.*
36 Mikhailin, "Vysshie formy – 'Za den' do nashei ery' Fedora Khitruka i Iuriia Norsteina."
37 *Gena the Crocodile* (1969), *Cheburashka* (1971), *Shapokliak* (1974), *Cheburashka Goes to School* (1983). Shvartsman's *Cheburashka* resulted from a revival of puppet animation experienced in the studio with the creation of the branch dedicated to traditional three-dimensional animation in 1952.
38 *Vinni Pukh* (1969), *Vinni Pukh idet v gosti* (1971), *Vinni Pukh i den' zabot* (1972). Other series with the beloved characters of Karlson, Maugli, the three from Prostokvashino or Leikin and Znaikina (in *At the Back Desk*) came out in only a few episodes. Only with *Just You Wait!* (*Nu Pogodi*, Viacheslav Kotenochkin, 1969–1993) did longer series start to be conceived. For the relevance and success of the series *Just You Wait!* among animated films of the time, see Vartanov, "Sekret uspekha."
39 Maliukova, "Poteriav, ne chuvstvoval sebia poteriannym."
40 Khitruk, *Professiia-animator*, 2007, 1: 291.
41 Khitruk, 1: 290–91.
42 Volkov, "S''est li volk zaitsa?," 131.
43 Maliukova, "Poteriav, ne chuvstvoval sebia poteriannym."
44 Followed by *Winnie the Pooh and Tigger Too* (1974), which was combined with the previous two in the feature-length movie *The Many Adventures of Winnie the Pooh* (1977).
45 Khitruk, *Professiia-animator*, 2007, 1: 190.
46 *The Spirit of Genius.*
47 Milne and Zakhoder, *Vinni-Pukh i vse ostal'nye.*
48 Volkov, "Razgovor o professii," 184.
49 Khitruk, *Professiia-animator*, 2007, 1: 190.
50 Khitruk, 1: 293.
51 Khitruk, 1: 191.
52 Khitruk, 1: 191.
53 Zuikov, "Vse reshila sluchainost'," 289.
54 Kostyukevich, "Rossiiskaia animatsiia v shkatulke s sekretom."
55 Khitruk, *Professiia-animator*, 2007, 1: 190.
56 Khitruk and Lukinykh, "Stepen' neveroiatnosti," 127.
57 Zuikov, "Vse reshila sluchainost'," 293.

58 Khitruk, *Professiia-animator*, 2007, 2: 293.
59 Nazarov, "Edik! Est' neplokhaia ideia…," 284.
60 Maliukova, "Poteriav, ne chuvstvoval sebia poteriannym."
61 Zuikov, "Vse reshila sluchainost'," 294.
62 Maliukova, "Poteriav, ne chuvstvoval sebia poteriannym."
63 See Tumelia's comment about the layout of music and sound for this film in Petrov and Tumelia, "Nauka udivliat'," 261.
64 *Fëdor Khitruk. Profession Animator.*
65 Elphick, "Vinni Pukh."
66 Elphick.
67 Khitruk, *Professiia-animator*, 2007, 1: 291.
68 Prokhorov, "Winnie-the-Pooh. Vinni Pukh," 301.
69 Khitruk, *Professiia-animator*, 2007, 1: 292.
70 Khitruk, 1: 192.
71 Khitruk and Lukinykh, "Stepen' neveroiatnosti," 128. Venzher, *Sotvorenie fil'ma*, 104.
72 Zuikov, "Vse reshila sluchainost'," 294–95.
73 Zuikov, 296.
74 Volkov, "Razgovor o professii," 184. On another occasion Khitruk tells how "Leonov swung pigeon-toed at the microphone, pouted and dangled his hand, just like Vinni Pukh!" Kapkov, "Golosa animatsii," 105. Once Leonov commented jokingly that Winnie the Pooh was one of his best roles. Maliukova, "Poteriav, ne chuvstvoval sebia poteriannym."
75 Zuikov, "Vse reshila sluchainost'," 294–95.
76 *The Spirit of Genius.*
77 Maliukova, "Poteriav, ne chuvstvoval sebia poteriannym."

Art and Society

3

Othello 67 (1967) and *Film, Film, Film* (1968)

In between *Bonifatius* and *Vinni Pukh* three films were made for an adult public, *The Man in the Frame* (see Chapter 2), *Othello 67*, and *Film Film Film*. Khitruk began to work on *Othello 67* after being invited to participate in the Expo 1967 in Montreal with a short inspired by the Expo theme "The Man and his World." The only condition for the submission was that the footage would not exceed a minute long.[1] Eventually, Khitruk's film together with eleven other selected shorts were compiled into one movie, *The World of Man*, by Albert Fisher.[2]

OTHELLO 67 (1967)

Sometimes the film is born from an image, sometimes from problems. And it is from problems that *Othello 67* was born.[3]

The idea for *Othello 67* was to represent a condensed version of Shakespeare's timeless drama. Portraying the tragedy in sixty seconds was a challenging task for Khitruk and art director Sergei Alimov; but at the end, they released a film that, more than about *Othello*, was a satirical comment on contemporary society; as Khitruk says, "it is a parody, a satire of the tendency to pack great pieces into convenient shapes."[4]

DOI: 10.1201/9781003199625-4

The film follows a trend of short films burgeoning in the 1960s, among which Khitruk seems mostly influenced by those made by Ion Popescu-Gopo. The Romanian director created films encapsulating stories condensed to an extreme already in the late 1950s (see his *Short History*, *Scurta istorie*, 1956); he then further matured a "theory of expressive synthesis"[5] that favored films in the form of animated sketches as short as fifteen seconds, which he would call "film-pills."[6] These laconic satirical miniatures presented poignant topical problems and sharp caricatures.[7] As in this trend, Khitruk presented an extremely abridged version of *Othello*, which becomes a parody not of the drama represented, but rather of the presentation of the drama itself. Despite its brevity, the film has a structure with a beginning, development, and resolution.[8] A driver arrives at a tollbooth, deposits a coin in a screen under the sign "Don't Waste Your Time," and in fifty seconds he consumes a sped-up version of Shakespeare's *Othello* (Figure 3.1).

As soon as the film ends, the spectator takes off and disappears in the same fast traffic and labyrinth of streets he came from (Figure 3.2).

FIGURE 3.1   *Othello 67.* Booth. © Soyuzmultfilm.

FIGURE 3.2 *Othello 67.* Labyrinth of streets. © Soyuzmultfilm.

The effect is quite humorous, although the critique is certainly explicit. The film, however, only hints at a deeper criticism of contemporary society that Khitruk would explore further in his later film *The Island* (1973).

As in all his animated films, the art director Alimov emphasized the conventionality of the images, eschewing a naturalistic representation of reality, focusing instead on conventionalized background, essential details and most of all flat figures. In *Othello 67*, Alimov and Khitruk follow this tendency in an extreme laconic way. The characters of the play turn into flat marionettes, their gestures are stylized and accelerated, and the dramatic action synthesized. A theatre stage functions as backdrop to the action; only its color shifts according to the change of act, which is delineated by fleeting titles. The stage is dotted with very limited details and a solid background that accentuates the flattening effect. The characters talk through the incomprehensible sound of a sped-up recording device and swift speech bubbles, which appear and disappear too fast to decode. The spectator does not have enough time to follow and understand what occurs on the screen, but the choice of colors in the background as well as in the characters' clothing conveys the mood of each act and underlines the nature of each character, especially the dark Iago (Figure 3.3).

Even the spectators at the booth look like the puppets on the screen, with their quick way of life. A parallel is drawn between the consumption

FIGURE 3.3   *Othello 67.* Theatre setting. © Soyuzmultfilm.

of culture in a pill form and a lifestyle that reaches such a level of speed that it turns the inhabitants into automatons. The film provides a surrogate of a tragedy obtaining a double effect on the original work by Shakespeare and its performance. Not only does a theatre staging, which is by nature not reproducible, become a mechanical reproduced commodity, but its condensed form amplifies the distance from the original play, doubting the value of the result. Thus, the film not only questions the mechanical reproducibility of a work of art in Benjaminian terms but offers a criticism on the reasoning behind any attempt to reduce works of art into a quickly consumable format. Besides, the method of consumption prevents the communal experience of the fruition of the work, reducing it to an isolated experience that does nothing but increasingly estrange the spectator in an already alienating society.

The challenge Khitruk undertook in making this extremely short film was not only a problem but became the theme of the work. Criticism on the speed and alienation that characterize modern society is a theme that will appear again in various forms in Khitruk's following films, the wittier and lighter of which is the one focused on the cinema world, *Film Film Film*, which followed soon after.

FILM FILM FILM (1968)

This is our [cinematic] happiness, and I wouldn't want another.

Genesis of the Film

When talking about the origin of this film, Khitruk recalls a speech delivered by Viktor Shklovsky, in which, after telling at length how he was banned, expelled, and forced to ever change his work, he ended with these words "This is our [cinematic] happiness, and I wouldn't want another."[9] Right there, the idea of *Film, Film, Film* began to take form in Khitruk's mind.

Khitruk shared with Shklovsky the same tireless creative drive as well as his concerns about the demands of the Soviet authorities over cinema, although he recognized that the pressure on the animation world seemed to be less exacting.[10] Indeed, despite the censorship, many artists and writers still found a refuge in animation after falling into disgrace with the authorities.[11]

Khitruk's embryonic idea of a film about the making of a movie evolved after a first-hand experience, when the director Stanislav Rostotskii entrusted the credits for one of his films to Khitruk's team. In the credits, each crew member was to be introduced by mini animated sequences expressing their role in a few traits. The project, ultimately, was not realized but Khitruk's conception of a future film began to evolve into concrete images.[12]

The opportunity to closely observe a live-action film production came with the request by the director El'dar Riazanov to create an animation insert at the beginning of his film *Zigzag of Success* (*Zigzag udachi*, 1968). For this task, Khitruk asked the artist Vladimir Zuikov to join the team. It was the first time Zuikov worked in animation and Khitruk saw this job as a chance to "train" him in the profession[13] (as seen in the previous chapter, Zuikov would then work for Khitruk's *Vinni Pukh* and subsequent films). The animation clip was successful and provided them with the occasion to gather many details about the activity at the studio Mosfil'm that later proved to be valuable for *Film Film Film*.[14]

The animated film opens with a panoramic view of the international cinema world in the form of photographs of famous directors, female movie stars (among them, Jayne Mansfield, Brigitte Bardot, Marilyn Monroe, and Sophia Loren) and representatives of the comedic world, especially Buster Keaton. Despite the initial focus on international celebrities, *Film Film Film*, however, turned out to have some specific Soviet connotations. The director in Khitruk's film, with his square face, close-distanced eyes, and disheveled hair, vaguely resembles Sergei Eisenstein. Khitruk fervently denied that he

made a parody of Eisenstein,[15] who was for him an "icon;"[16] and insisted
that in his mind Eisenstein was different from the director depicted in *Film
Film Film*, not only in his physique, but also in demeanor. Perhaps, he noted,
the director in the film was closer in look and explosive temperament to the
director Grigorii Roshal',[17] or some of his gestures, like holding his chin in
deep thoughts, could recall Stanislavsky.[18] Nazarov, instead, says it was the
features of the animation director Lev Mil'chin that inspired the character's
appearance.[19] Wherever the truth lies, Khitruk's main intention was to find a
general, emblematic figure of the directorial profession.

   Still, a few scenes of *Film Film Film* are clearly a tribute to Eisenstein's
Ivan the Terrible, from Nikolai Cherkasov's distinctive pointed beard sticking
up in the air from the coffin in Holbein's style[20] (Figure 3.4), to the procession
of the *oprichniki* in the cathedral (Figure 3.5).

   The choice of *Ivan the Terrible* also ties well with the scene about censorship, as it is well known that Eisenstein himself endured difficult relations
with censors (Figure 3.6).

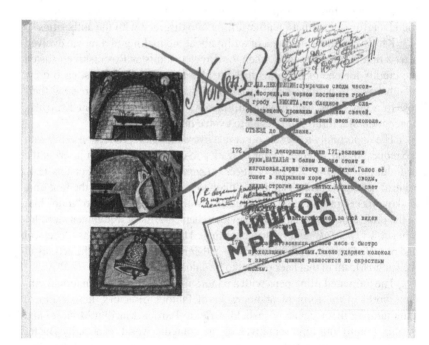

FIGURE 3.4   *Film Film Film*. Ivan's beard and censorship for dark scene. Cel.
© Soyuzmultfilm.

FIGURE 3.5   *Film Film Film*. *Oprichniki* procession. © Soyuzmultfilm.

Khitruk not only was influenced by Eisenstein, but he also shared with him several traits. As the Eisenstein historian Naum Kleiman comments, both directors created an art that is visually very expressive, they aimed to enlighten and educate and they both respected Disney's craft and dynamism, as well his ability to bring together images and music.[21]

Musical Refrain

In all of Khitruk's films, music plays an important role; it accompanies actions, sets the tone, and underlies the shifts of mood in the dramatic play. In this film, the music created by the composers Aleksandr Zatsepin and Evgenii Krylatov also unifies the individual episodes, and, most importantly, constitutes a layer on which the entire parody is structured. At the beginning of the film, a catchy song eulogizing the effervescent and cheerful cinema world accompanies a series of colored, or brightly tinted, photographs of actors, cameramen, and directors. The refrain will also resound throughout the film at the end of each episode, emphasizing the climatic point while contributing to link the independent episodes. The upbeat tone of the song suits the lyrics comparing the cinema realm to a magical and sweet dream; but soon, with the very first animated frame of the film, the joyful images abruptly clash. The smiling and glamorous faces of the celebrities in the photographs give

FIGURE 3.6 *Film Film Film*. Censorship. Cel. © Soyuzmultfilm.

way to the sunken cheeks and emaciated body of a suffering scriptwriter at his typing machine. Instead of the preceding flashy colors, a block of ash grey constitutes the only background. The absence of lines delimiting the floor, walls, or ceiling, places the distraught scriptwriter in a grey vacuum which accurately reflects his inner feelings (Figure 3.7).

The tone of the music undergoes a dramatic change from the opening song; now, only string cords play an ominous theme while the scriptwriter paces back and forth.

FIGURE 3.7   *Film Film Film*. Scriptwriter. © Soyuzmultfilm. Subtitles Films by Jove.

The caricatured vignette of writer's block is delineated in a few crucial strokes: the essential expressions of the character's face, his scarce but telling gestures, the rhythm created by his mood swings, and the use of symbols, such as a thread of smoke turning into a noose tightening up around his neck as an ultimate symbol of his despair. This scene is reminiscent of the opening of a 1963 film *Jealousy* (*Revnost*) by the Bulgarian director Todor Dinov, revealing once again an exchange of ideas among the animators of the Eastern Bloc. In Dinov's film, a composer (stylized but much more angular than Khitruk's caricatured scriptwriter) is depicted at his piano plunged in a creative process. In the very first scene of both works, the caricatured artists, together with a clever use of music and symbolism, already exhibit the humorous tone that would reign in the film.

Sources of the Comic

If the musical refrain provides a glorious image of the cinematic realm against which reality clashes, the screenwriter's peculiar position in the same world offers another layer of the parody. Once at the studio, the writer experiences the fictional reality that surrounds him from an outsider's point of view, his consequent shocked reaction to unlikely encounters and unexpected events becomes a successful source of laughter (see when a skeleton asks him to light a cigarette).

The scriptwriter's first encounter with the space of the studio appears as a visual projection of his feelings – a stair leads him into some infernal depth, and a labyrinth of paths and barriers, similar to the intricate net of streets in *Othello 67*, entrap and disorient him (Figures 3.8 and 3.9).

At the end, he finds himself locked in a lift, separated from the rest of the team in every sense, his creation now in the hands of the director. At this point, the film switches to the director's point of view, and the screenwriter will appear again only in the last scene and during the scrolling of the final credits, as a framing device for the film.

The screenwriter is perhaps the most successful caricature in the film, but the image of the director also contributes to the comic effect. He is defined with exaggerated traits and habits that are all the more humorous when they repeat – see his face changing color in moments of rage or his recurring consumption of valium. Gestures and their repetitions acquire a marked quality in this film since, much as in silent movies, there are no spoken words, and pantomime reigns.

As in previous films, instead of a language code, sounds are used to express characters' words and their feeling. Words come only in written forms: to label the role of a character (see again Figure 3.7) or to illustrate the intrusion of censorship into the creative work. Labeling the nameless heroes provides a generalized conception of the characters as representatives of their professional class as a whole. Names are not important, it is the characters' function, their role, that is fundamental. This generalization, rather than focus on a Soviet eulogy of work classes, raises the story to a universal level to include the common challenges within the creative world. Besides, the

FIGURE 3.8   *Film Film Film*. Director and scriptwriter descending the stairs. © Soyuzmultfilm.

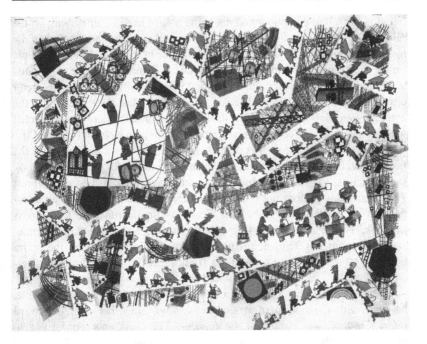

FIGURE 3.9 *Film Film Film*. Labyrinth of paths. © Soyuzmultfilm.

labeling creates a humorous effect by offering an unnecessary explanation of each character's role already evident from the image.

The origin of the comic lies not only in the caricatured way the protagonists are depicted or the peculiar use of words, but also, in the use of well-proven tricks from comedic films, in Khrzhanovskii's words, "a true anthology of comedy craftsmanship."[22] Acceleration of the rhythm, visual gags, comic situations and repetitions abound.

The film runs on an accelerated rhythm punctuated by the beat of the refrain. The rhythm suits the race against time the director experiences in order to produce the film within the budget and recreates the stressful atmosphere. Sudden pauses effectively interrupt the overall sped-up pace and only add to the humorous outcome.

As in the unfailing slapstick tradition, visual gags and repetitions are an effective source of laughter. In this film, visual gags are based on the spectator's feeling of disrupted expectations (the audience does not expect an army of extras coming out of a small van), or incongruity of the events (the shooting stops to wait for the arrival of a tank of water to create artificial rain only to have a real downpour and not being able to use it). Repetitions, on the other hand, build up tension and then offer a release. In the scene when the historical character Malyuta Skuratov throws the hero down the cliff multiple times, each repetition intensifies the spectators' sympathy for the mistreated actor, and then turns their compassion into laughter with the undaunted actor climbing the stairs each time. The gag is topped by a last shift: eventually, the actor playing Malyuta satisfies the director, he throws the hero down the cliff with the necessary intensity – next frame the hero is in a coffin (Figure 3.10).

The tint of black humor is dispelled by the conscious realization of the fictional reality, even more so as the scene continues with the director coaxing the actress to express her mourning with exaggerated histrionic gestures. The series of gags does not end here, but reaches the climax with an unexpected ring, a call of reprimand from Goskino admonishing that "the scene is too dark." (see again Figure 3.4) In a swift change of scene in a puppet-theater style, the mourning sequence is turned into a wedding banquet, the coffin becomes a table, the hero resuscitates from the coffin and is dressed in ceremonial clothes, and the weeping wife becomes a merry bride (Figure 3.11).

The coffin and then the banquet with the unmistakable swan on the table, together with the discourse around censorship, are other straightforward references to Eisenstein's *Ivan the Terrible*. The Goskino's request is also an allusion to the forced positive ending imposed on Khitruk in *Man in the*

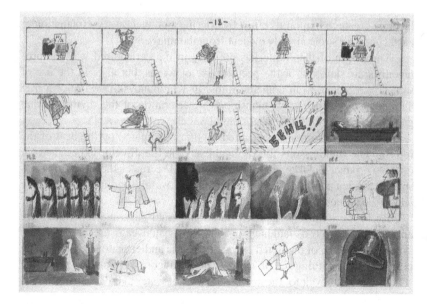

FIGURE 3.10   *Film Film Film*. Malyuta's scene. Storyboard. © Soyuzmultfilm.

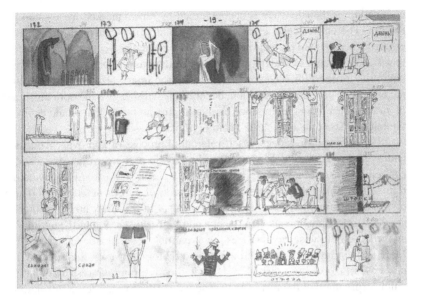

FIGURE 3.11 *Film Film Film*. Mourning to wedding scene. Storyboard.
© Soyuzmultfilm.

Frame,[23] which inexorably followed the persistent demand to present a joyful and ideal depiction of reality according to the socialist realist mandate.

Censorship

The censorship process is addressed even more blatantly at the beginning of the film, when the director and the scriptwriter embark on the adventure of having the script approved. With humor and wit Khitruk depicts the director running in and out of offices along the side of a corridor, the length of which underlines the feeling of the endless bureaucratic process. We do not see what happens behind the doors – a parallel to the absurd inhabitants of a similar corridor in George Dunning's *Yellow Submarine* suggests another layer of parody – however, we see the effect of the bureaucratic system in the director's face, in his reactions, as well as in the form of various laconic and often contradictory stamps on the script itself. A similar succession of doors also appeared in Khitruk's film *Man in the Frame*; but the dark scene in the older film turns here into a humorous vignette despite the serious underlying topic.

The comic effect springs from the whimsical situations and the use of music. The frenzied run of the two characters in and out of doors, moving forward and sometimes backward on the corridor leading toward the completion of their journey is accompanied by music marked by a sped-up rhythm. The entire scene is constructed on pantomime canons of the silent-era, from accelerated projection to humorous visual gags – it is not by chance that Buster Keaton is widely represented in the passing photographs at the beginning of the film. The scene resolves in the image of an ornate door at the end of the corridor. Its position, decoration, and size give the door an aura of awe and fear as in the presence of an almighty authority that would decide the fate of these two artists (see again Figure 3.6).

This meta scene reflects a self-referential process of approvals Khitruk had to go through in order to have his film, and in particular this very scene, cleared. In the original script, the Muse that appears at the beginning would return here only to be covered by a multitude of censoring stamps.[24] The historian of animation, Borodin, points out that in the Goskino's files there is a recommendation to shorten the episode "at the discretion of the authors" as the length of the scene "violates the dynamics of the plot development."[25] More than a suggestion concerning plot and rhythm, however, this seemed to be a case of censoring censorship. Despite the disappointing restriction, it is quite surprising that the rest of the scene was still allowed. Yet, Khitruk did not understand the necessity of this cut, as truly he did not comprehend many other instances in which films were "shelved," he indeed believed that even those in the "shelf commission" would often forget the reason.[26]

Tackling the issue of censorship was also a topic dear to the screenwriter of *Film, Film, Film*, Vladimir Golovanov, who himself experienced its impact on his career. The playwright Aleksandr Timofeevskii recalls how Golovanov's early scripts, written when still attending VGIK, were brought to Soyuzmultfilm but remained unrealized for not fitting into the canons of socialist realism of that time. Golovanov was eventually expelled from VGIK for his insubordinate attitude and actions. *Film Film Film* was the only script – according to Timofeevskii, not very typical for Golovanov – adopted at that time.[27]

It was not the first time for Khitruk to be intrigued by Golovanov's scripts. After *Story of a Crime*, one of his scripts, *The Death of the Passenger*, caught his attention. The story recalled the style of *Man in the Frame*, although "the content was closer to the theater of the absurd."[28] Obviously, it was risky to venture into such experimental work; not only the Artistic Council "killed the script"[29] but also the renowned film director Sergei Yutkevich and the cartoonist and director Boris Efimov suggested that Khitruk refuse to work on the script. Khitruk himself admits that he felt there was an "internal censor" inside him who kept repeating "they will not allow it."[30] In his biography Khitruk bitterly regrets his decision not to fight for this script and his choice to be on the safe side.[31] This regret was perhaps even more distressing because many of Golovanov's early scripts suffered the same fate.

With *Film Film Film*, Golovanov cautiously dipped his toe in the water with a safe and entertaining, rather than complex and sophisticated, script. As Khitruk notices during the discussion of the literary script, "we did not want to do a satire, because we were a little tired of it, but to speak simply, we wanted to do a light, simple comedy, an acting comedy."[32] Later, in the discussion of the theme of the film, Khitruk clarifies,

> The film is conceived as a buffoonery, in the style of old Mack Sennett comedies. Hustle and bustle, wild hassle and the very falsification of cinematic life serve only as a pretext for creating all sorts of comic collisions and transformations.[33]

Indeed, the film is entertaining; still, as in any other film by Khitruk, much more can be read through the frames.

NOTES

1 Khitruk, *Professiia-animator*, 1: 188.
2 See https://expo-67.ca/en/albert-fisher-the-world-of-man/
3 Khitruk, *Professiia-animator*, 1: 188.
4 Khitruk, 1: 189.
5 Bendazzi, *Animation*, 2: 71.
6 Bendazzi, 2: 71.
7 One could see these films together with Khitruk's *Othello 67* as the predecessors of the Cuban Padrón's "filminuto" of the 1980s.
8 Khitruk, *Professiia-animator*, 1: 188.
9 Shklovsky's words quoted in Khitruk, 1: 184.
10 Khitruk, 1: 184.
11 *Fëdor Khitruk. Portrait of An Artist and His Era. Film 9.*
12 Volkov, "Razgovor o professii," 184.
13 Volkov, 184.
14 Volkov, 184.
15 Khitruk recalls, "For some misunderstanding, critics came to the conclusion that I did a parody of Eisenstein, this is absolutely not true. Whenever I can, I sharply retort against it, I deny it. I didn't have in mind Eisenstein, it was simply a coincidence that my director was making a historical film." (i186)
16 Maliukova, "Poteriav, ne chuvstvoval sebia poteriannym."
17 Maliukova.
18 "'Fil'm Fil'm Fil'm.' Literaturnyi Stsenarii F. S. Khitruka, V. A. Golovanova. Varianty," 16.
19 *Miracle Factory. Part 3 Art Director.*
20 See Eisenstein's sketch in Tsivian, *Ivan the Terrible*, 40 and his comparison with Holbein the Younger, *The Body of the Dead Christ in the Tomb.*

21 Naum Kleiman's interview in *The Spirit of Genius*.
22 Khrzhanovskii, "Fyodor Khitruk," 37.
23 The discussion on the ending is discussed in the chapter relative to the film *Man in the Frame*.
24 "Animation from A to Z. Film 9."
25 Borodin, "Animatsiia podnevol'naia." ch.5, 22.
26 "Animation from A to Z. Film 9."
27 Borodin, "Animatsiia podnevol'naia." ch.6 p.31.
28 Khitruk, *Professiia-animator*, 1: 168.
29 Maliukova, "Poteriav, ne chuvstvoval sebia poteriannym."
30 Maliukova.
31 Khitruk, *Professiia-animator*, 1: 168.
32 "Stenogramma zasedaniia khudozhdestvennogo soveta po obsuzhdeniiu literaturnogo stsenarii F. Khitruka, V. Golovanova '*Fil'm fil'm fil'm*,'" 29.
33 "'*Fil'm Fil'm Fil'm*.' Literaturnyi Stsenarii F. S. Khitruka, V. A. Golovanova. Varianty," 2.

Individual and Society

4

The Island (1973), *I'll Give You a Star* (1974), and *Icarus and the Wisemen* (1976)

Once *Film Film Film* was released, Khitruk returned to films for children with the series of Winnie the Pooh (*Vinni Pukh*) discussed in previous chapters. This three-episode series would be his last directorial work for young audiences. In between the episodes and especially after *Vinni Pukh*'s last film was released, Khitruk invested his efforts in those topical or philosophical themes that were most dear to him and produced a few films with a focus on the individual vis-à-vis society. The first film following the completion of the Winnie the Pooh series, *The Island* (1973), presents the story of a castaway as an image of a single person's position in modern society, the following *I'll Give You a Star* (1974) explores the eternal woman question, while *Icarus* (1976) celebrates freedom and the right to be different and unique.

DOI: 10.1201/9781003199625-5

THE ISLAND (OSTROV, 1973)

The story of this award-winning film revolves around a castaway, a new Robinson, stranded on a little island with only the company of a palm tree. Passersby approach the island from all directions, without saving the shipwrecked man; until at the end, another castaway swims by, and together they leave.

The theme of isolation of the individual is a recurrent theme in the animation of the 1970s, in both children's and adult works. In the children's films, as Beumers pointed out,

> the late 1960s and 1970s show the individual as increasingly isolated from society. The collective has collapsed. In cartoons of the stagnation the child's loneliness becomes a focal point. Children are viewed as isolated and misunderstood, both by society and their parents.[1]

The young characters eventually reconnect to their parents by teaching them a lesson, as seen in Khitruk's earlier *Toptyzhka*, and also in Kachanov's *Varezhka* and Popov's series of the *Three from Prostokvashino*, among the most successful films. Alternatively, as for ex. in Cheburashka, children abandon their isolation to be reintegrated into society at large thanks to the intervention of friends. Similarly, in Khitruk's *The Island*, the castaway moves out of his confinement when he finds a kindred soul, and together they swim toward a utopic horizon.

The film tackles societal criticism on various grounds. It aligns with a general tendency in these years to bring to the fore actual problems – from anti-war films to defense of the environment – in order to influence and educate the audience.[2] Among those films with an anti-war theme, it is worth mentioning a 1973 short *Balance of Fear* (*Ravnovesie strakha*), not only because it was created by the same team Khitruk-Nazarov-Zuikov – and here Nazarov acted as the main director, while Khitruk fulfilled more of a supervisor role and modestly appears in the credit at a third place – but also because the directors explore in the film a similar condensation of a theme in a short time (here only two minutes) as in *Othello 67* and the concise visual style and accelerated rhythm adopted for *The Island*. In *Balance of Fear*, as in the famous Norman McLaren's film *Neighbours* (1952), two peaceful neighbors come to a conflict which escalates to their own destruction.

The topic was particularly relevant in these decades of ongoing Cold War and animators were keen on promoting dialogues between the two sides of the Iron Curtain. In an attempt to foster communication between animators from both sides, an association was founded in 1960, ASIFA – the International Animated Film Association, of which Khitruk was an early member and, in the 1980s, also its vice-president.

As an ASIFA member, Khitruk had opportunities to attend festivals and come into contact with international animation.[3] It was time, he thought, to bring Soviet animation into the discussion. Inspired by contemporary films such as *Operation x-70* by Raoul Servais (1971) or *The Snails* (*Les Escargots*) by René Laloux (1966), which he considered examples of "civic energy," Khitruk promoted a political and social commitment in animation.[4] He strived to foster collaborations among animators from all the Republics in the Soviet Union, as well as creative exchanges among animators from different countries, with a particular emphasis on the socialist Eastern European countries.[5]

A social and political approach was not new for Soviet animation, it was a return to the role of animation of the 1920s and 1930s and of the war years; this time, though, it was endowed with a new language fit for topical problems; in Khitruk's words, "today's political films, political poster have to be realized with a language of contemporary art, [...] a contemporary problem requires its own language."[6] Instead of returning to the aesthetic of the 1920s–30s – as for example in the contemporary films *Peace to Your House* (*Mir domu tvoemu*, Nikolaev, Nikitin, 1962) or *It is in Our Power* (*Eto v nashikh silakh*, Atamanov, 1970) – Khitruk opted for a style that recalls films from the so called Zagreb School (where "school" stands more for a unified frame of mind of the animators gathering around Zagreb Films, than a school per se). *The Island*, as Norstein would say, evokes the style of the Yugoslav animation with "Khitruk's intonation."[7]

Caricature Style

While the Zagreb animators' styles widely differed, they shared a meticulous choice of expressive details, laconic forms, and philosophical and topical themes condensed in brief scenes. Films by Vukotić, Mimica, Dovniković, Zaninović, to name only a few representatives, often deal with the fate of man in contemporary, dehumanizing culture. In particular, two films strike as influential for Khitruk's *The Island*: Ante Zaninović's *The Wall* (*Zid*, 1966), and Borivoj (Bordo) Dovniković's film *Curiosity* (*Znatiželja*, 1966). *The Wall*, a type of philosophical parable in a concise form, presents a character aesthetically very similar to Khitruk's castaway; *Curiosity* has a similar structure as *The Island*, with the lone protagonist in the center of the screen, approached by visitors merely interested in the content of a bag laid next to him on the bench.[8]

The sharp, geometrical characters of the 1960s now turn to simple contour lines that recall caricatures from newspapers and journals. As often found in the Zagreb School films, the comic quality arises from the condensed situations, exaggeration of the details, and absurd situations that compete with a critical commentary on society. Khitruk here employs similar devices to widen the humor to include a harsher comment on contemporary reality already present in *Film, Film, Film.*

As in previous films, Khitruk, Zuikov, and Nazarov rejected the naturalistic representation of the characters and opted instead for a caricatured rendition of the protagonists, choosing telling details in their external depiction as well as in the phases of movements. In *The Island*, Khitruk's team bring these concepts to the extreme and the protagonist is stripped bare to simple traits. A plain line for the feet functions as base for an oversized head, complete with a mass of hair turning into a long beard that covers the entire naked body. His nakedness places him in a conception of generalization, his hair and beard point to his situation (stranded on an island), his long nose gives a sense of a face behind the hairy cover, his eyes are defined by dark dots, which assume an incredible power of expression[9] (Figure 4.1).

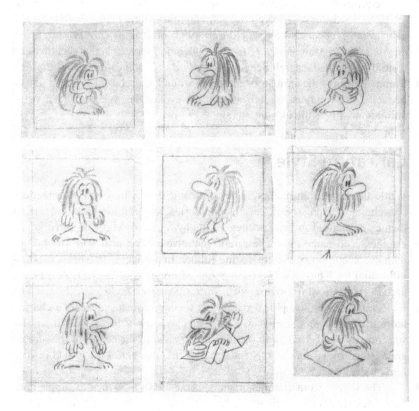

FIGURE 4.1   *The Island.* Castaway. Model sheet. © Soyuzmultfilm.

Topical Themes

The film tackles many issues, each one presented in the form of a visit from the world outside the solitary island. The passing boats are characters themselves; they have their own personality and gait, now slow and sleepy, then fast and busy, or later bubbly and superficial. All of them act unilaterally with the hero, they do not interact with him, rather they act upon him. They are the subject of the action, whereas the hero is only a passive object, equitable to the palm tree at the center of the island, visited, exploited, and left to die.

Each encounter of our Robinson with the external world introduces a new theme and criticism of modern society. Some of the ideas adopted for the episodes drew from material first gathered by the team for a satirical film against Western lifestyle, *The Wild West*, which had just been disappointedly interrupted at the script stage. Allegedly, the work on this film was suspended because of the warming of the relations between USSR and America following the visit of President Nixon to Moscow, which made a political pamphlet less desirable.[10] Still, part of the material for this film was used for the short *The Balance of Fear*, and some more for *The Island*. Despite the seriousness of the criticism and the themes suggested in these films, Khitruk, together with Zuikov and Nazarov, employ witty devices that inspire, if not laughter, at least a smile.

The source of the comic lies in the incongruity of the encounters; with each scene Khitruk sets up the expectation of the hero's salvation, only to be frustrated by the visitors' incongruous acts and sudden disappearance. Each visit is built on quick interventions, often using exaggerated details and repetition as comic devices. The extreme speed of the unfolding events and the sudden departure, together with the absurd situation contribute to heightening the parody and trigger a reaction founded in both laughter and pity. The hero is caught off-guard, his stumped expression resonates with the spectators, who laugh a Pirandellian "riso amaro" realizing the selfish tragedy intrinsic in the depicted modern society.

The comic tone of the film is not only obtained through the ever-increasing pace and absurdity of the situations, but also through repetitive gags. Repetition provokes laughter, as well as underlines the castaway's hopelessness. It is also employed to emphasize the comic quality of unexpected elements, such as the humorous recurrent appearance of a periscope, which tones down a disquieting feeling of surveillance. The big cartoonish blinking eyes popping out of the periscope lenses also contribute to the comic effect (Figure 4.2).

Only when scenes of war jolt out from a newspaper article folded in boat shape does the presence of the submarine acquire a more sinister connotation. Scenes of violence springing out of the newspaper page intermingle with

FIGURE 4.2 *The Island.* Periscope. © Soyuzmultfilm.

pictures of fashion, titles in foreign languages and words pointing to goods and money. A comment on the senselessness of war, the brainwashing bombardment of consumerism, as well as the detrimental effect of the media on our minds is conveyed with quickly alternating images that literally assault the hero, as well as the audience, through devices such as stroboscopic lights, alternating colors, collages, simulated camera movements, and Eisenstein-like dynamic editing. This dark commentary is soon followed by a lighter tone presented by a festive wheel steamboat passing by (of course without stopping).

Khitruk mocks all spheres of society and art; each boat provides a condensed characterization of that sphere; reporters take interviews and then leave him behind, scientists study him as a rare species and then abandon him, tourists take pictures with him before they depart, and a seller submerges him with a pile of consumer goods that he could hardly use on the island, before disappearing as fast as he appeared.

Khitruk's team does not even spare topics such as irresponsible fishing and art smuggling, both issues presented in a humorous way through a parody of chase scenes in action movies. If the fishing of a whale turns into a shooting scene, the art smuggling scene loads the police chase with comic gags: a thief passes by with the stolen Michelangelo's *Dying Slave*; Interpol follows and picks up Robinson to help them; once the police arrest the thief, they

FIGURE 4.3 *The Island*. Interpol scene. © Soyuzmultfilm.

reward our hero for his help with a coin and … return him to the island. As an additional climax of the absurd circumstances, the thief, while passing by behind bars, manages to steal the same coin from the abandoned hero[11] (Figure 4.3).

Another scene attacks the church, a topic often used in Soviet satire of all times. Not even Christian compassion is the source of Robinson's salvation; the boat in the shape of a cathedral (emerging from an aptly tinted ecclesiastical purple) will leave our hero with a blessing and a Bible. An interesting Soviet commentary follows: the periscope resurfaces, looks suspiciously at the hero, and makes him drop the Gospel.

Topics touched on by the films also encompass attacks on colonialism and environmental issues. The first point materializes in the form of a battleship advancing toward the foreground (a visual image borrowed from the ship in Eisenstein's *Battleship Potemkin*), from which captain and sailors disembark to the island, raise a new flag, give a salute, fire a cannon ball, and disappear. The island is conquered, the inhabitants are not important.

Finally, international oil exploitation will mark the end of the island. If at the beginning sailors come to cut down the only palm tree Robinson has, now the hero can only sit on the top of the drill, and instead of the island there is a large oil stain.

Sound and Rhythm

Khitruk usually starts working on a new project by creating before all else the "timing," that is the rhythmic structure for his scenes, on which he then records dialogue and music; first of all he needs to "hear" his film.[12] However, for *The Island*, he began to make the film without a phonogram, and it was only when he watched the draft montage that he realized how much the film dragged.[13] The single scenes seemed to please him, but once put together, the film was falling short. The story goes that by chance, while watching the film at the editing table, Khitruk inadvertently sped up the projection one and a half notch faster. The accident suddenly revealed the necessary tempo! The film was about contemporary civilization with its insane rhythm; and it was this very crazy rhythm that was missing. A simple chance event got them out of the impasse, and finally, Khitruk recalls, "the film was breathing as expected."[14]

The acceleration suits the overall goal of representing a non-naturalistic and condensed version of reality; it constitutes an additional layer of manipulation in the hands of the animator.[15] On the one hand, the increased speed manipulates time in a way that affects not only the rhythm of the film, but ultimately the perception of the film in a comic, parodic way. On the other hand, this device substitutes the need for spoken words through a cinematic language that transcends speech. As in *Othello 67*, dialogue here is substituted by another code of communication with the spectator made of only accelerated sounds. The literary layer of the film is replaced by a cinematic or, more precisely, a technological layer, which emphasizes the overall discourse on modern society. Although the criticism seems to encompass society at large, often a certain intonation indicating the English language can be distinguished in the visitors' gibberish, a strategy that was commonly used to narrow down the critique to the capitalist society (see also in *I'll Give You a Star*).

Sound participates in the composition of rhythm, sets the mood, acts as a substitute for words, and offers an interpretative key. It also provides an element of characterization for each boat and even acquires a dramatic function; the oil sucking from the island in a pulsing motion resounds like a heartbeat that slows down to a stop until all signs of life are gone and; a sense of doom pervades the scene with Robinson sitting in silence on the drill in the middle of an oil atoll. Also the off-screen sound has a peculiar role; it amplifies a sense of expectation, while it also refers to a vast reality beyond the reach of the hero, which makes the theme of isolation of the individual in modern society even more acute. When the image and sound finally reunite on the screen (the boat appears), no relief follows, and the hero's expectation, shared by the audience, is frustrated by the indifference of the visitors. At times, the sound is incongruent with the image that follows, thus creating a comic effect, as when a tiny, short-tailed tugboat appears on the screen after being preceded by a booming rattle that prepares the audience for a much larger vessel.

Often, loud noises accompany the images and contribute to the overwhelming feeling the hero experiences – from the noise of heavy transportation or loud music and entertainment, to sounds of bombs, intermingled with high-paced reporters' announcements. To these assaulting noises coming from modern society, Khitruk juxtaposes the complete silence of the island. This silence, although short-lived, denies any comfort, but rather amplifies the oppressive loneliness and isolation that the hero experiences.

Only at the end is a low comforting sound heard. Once again, it comes from outside the frame. It breaks the desperate silence in the form of a gentle whistle followed by a single swimming man, a visual castaway twin for our hero, who beckons Robinson to join him. The two leave together sharing a broken mast, at first zig zagging uncertainly, looking for an accord, until they find harmony in the same rhythm, and together they swim away (Figure 4.4).

Their departure is accompanied by the calm and soothing, although melancholic, female singing voice with which the film opens. The soundtrack (composed by Shandor Kallosh) creates a frame for the film and suggests a message of hope, despite the challenges, for connection on a human level, reachable with mutual understanding.

FIGURE 4.4 *The Island.* Two Robinsons. © Soyuzmultfilm.

Representation of Time and Space

Only when the castaway-double comes to the rescue do the boundaries of the island open up to a wide stretch of water and a shared swimming path. Until then, the space encircling the island reveals merely isolation. Its boundaries are only violated by external forces. The space is permeable as much as Robinson is a victim; by acting on him, the world annihilates his space.

The unusual approach of making the protagonist a passive figure reflects in the organization of space, as well as the representation of time. The visits follow one another in independent episodes and the consequent fragmentation of linear time contributes to the overall feeling of disorientation. This feeling is heightened by the in-between moments when the hero finds himself alone on the island. The passing of time in isolation and solitude is simply realized with a depiction of the hero sitting still, holding his knees into his chest, the only movement visible is his blinking eyes. It is this very little detail, the blinking of the eyes, that gives meaning to the wait, transforming a static image into a representation of helpless waiting. The fact that the hero repetitively goes back to the same position, frozen in the same static frame throughout most of the film, reinforces the message. Time can also stretch to infinity, like when a ship without a single person on board passes by, like the "Flying Dutchman."[16] The legend of the ghost ship doomed to sail the oceans forever appears here as a sinister omen for the hero.

The image of the island, in the very center of the frame, represents the present time. Boats often cross the frame from left to right, going from past to future, while Robinson is centered in the middle, stuck in the present, separated from the past and not knowing what the future will bring. He also seems to call for a moment of reflection between past actions and future consequences, as in the scene with two boats carrying cars, the one passing from left to right carries brand new cars, the one from right to left – a garbage pile full of scrapped cars (Figure 4.5).

Only at the end is the hero able to move forward; he leaves the island with the new friend, swimming toward the horizon, on an alternative route toward an uncertain but timidly hopeful future.

I'LL GIVE YOU A STAR (DARIU TEBE ZVEZDU, 1974)

If *The Island* offers a promising hint of a brighter future, the following film, *I'll Give You a Star*, instead seems to underline the character's doom. With this film, Khitruk attempts to present the question of woman's role in

FIGURE 4.5 *The Island.* Cars and garbage. © Soyuzmultfilm.

society with wit and humor; however, the script, written by Mariia Motruk, Khitruk's wife and a long-time animator at Soyuzmultfilm, betrays an underlying sense of helplessness. The plot unfolds around the figure of a woman who reappears throughout different eras, each time being promised stars and idolization, but each time ending up subserviently attending to her man.

Once more, Zuikov and Nazarov worked in tandem as art directors and developed a style similar to *The Island* and still influenced by the Zagreb school manner: movements are simplified, characters are caricatured and conveyed with few traits, and a narrator's commentary ties the separate episodes. Valentin Nikulin's matter-of-fact but still engaging narration describes the events from the cave era, through the Middle Ages, then modern day, and finally a futuristic time. While his voice accompanies images on the screen, each scene provides those extra details that present a hilarious commentary on the narration. Repetition elicits a comic effect, especially with the recurrence throughout the times of a brass pot that each woman ends up cleaning. The accompanying sound of the scourging pot reinforces the symbol of her eternal exploitation and the doom of the woman's condition (Figure 4.6).

FIGURE 4.6   *I'll Give You a Star.* Harem and pot. Sketch. © Soyuzmultfilm.

Concrete Time and Space

While the film spans through four different eras, it also addresses contemporary reality. Busy and hectic modern life transpires through pulsing lights and quick montage. Speedy cars flicker on the intersecting highways just as in *Othello 67*. The man's clothes and hairstyle, as well as the consumer goods in the apartment, concretize the 1970s era (Figure 4.7).

The narrative voice resounds over the character's speaking English, as though the slight criticism on contemporary life is not directed toward the Soviet society, but American capitalist society instead – a device often employed to camouflage a wider criticism and at the same time reaffirm a socialist tradition. The co-presence of the two languages, while asserting a foreign location, also alludes to the universality of the problem.

Flaws in the Whole

The single gags and the idea of the recurrent brass pot as a symbol of women's destiny and exploitation are successful, but the film in its whole is lacking a spark that would make it more appealing. Khitruk himself could

FIGURE 4.7 *I'll Give You a Star.* The man's apartment. © Soyuzmultfilm.

not pinpoint the reason for what he calls his "biggest flop;"[17] "for some reason," he says, "the film did not flow rhythmically or even narratively," it lacked "those very points that should create a certain state of euphoria in the auditorium."[18]

Khitruk's team enjoyed the process of making the film, "how we liked all this while we were doing it! Every detail!" Khitruk says, "It seemed to me that all of this was funny. And how Valentin Nikulin voiced!"[19] But once they saw the final version of the film on screen, Khitruk was very disappointed, "literary my belly froze,"[20] he says. The film received awards, such as the prestigious Special Jury Prize for short films at Cannes Film Festival in 1975, but Khitruk was still very dissatisfied with it, "This film traumatized me. It received some prizes, and it is shown regularly on March 8, but for me it was a trauma."[21]

Zuikov also considers this work his most unsuccessful film; perhaps, he ventures, because the topic was not undertaken with the necessary breadth and, consequently, the superficial approach also affected the visual plane.[22]

Woman Question

The film clearly presents a sharp, although humorous, criticism of men's attitude toward women, but does not delve into the topic in depth, and, from a traditional feminist point of view, this leads to some consideration. The woman is represented in her attractive forms, her prominent breast and pronounced hips emphasize her being a "spectacle," a subject of the male gaze and desire, even more so as she is devoid of words or facial expressions. Following the man, she is reduced to a beautiful object, literally picked up and idolized, and then put to work. While the film offers a criticism of gender-based representation of women and ridicules assumptions around the "woman's role," it depicts the female character in a way that reinforces the stereotypes. The comic outcome from comedy based on stereotypes usually comes with sympathy for the subject, but in this film the spectators cannot fully empathize with the spouse, perhaps because the film positions the woman as the helpless, passive figure, not only unable to rebel against the situation, but also unable to desire an active change; or maybe because her existence seems to be justified by her desire to be desired, as though her justification for being is dependent on the man.

In a more specific Soviet context, the film lacks any reference to the position of the Soviet woman as a bearer of double burden, as worker and housekeeper, but it becomes even more humorous in the light of the propaganda discourse of emancipation of the Soviet women. Historically, the women's role in the kitchen was perceived as the utmost sign of their exploitation. Lenin's wish that "every cook needs to learn to rule the state," found significant force in the propaganda of the 1920s.[23] The emancipation of the woman from the kitchen, a topic that regained force in the Khrushchev's years preceding this film, was strictly related to principles of modernization, efficiency, and technology.[24] Now, in this 1970s' film, the old pot, the same throughout the ages, wittingly points to the failure of an official discourse preoccupied with identifying social progress with scientific and technological progress.

The theoretical equalitarian stance to emancipate women from the kitchen proved to be only a utopia, with a consequent resignation of Soviet women over the years, or in Boym's words, "a stoic position taken by the majority of Russian working women who do not believe that Russian men could undergo any kind of mental perestroika."[25] Perhaps this is the very message of the film.

Anima-genic

Khitruk observed that the script was compelling but not easily realizable in animation terms, it was not "anima-genic" (*mul'tigenichen*).[26] Similar to Epstein's *photogénie*,[27] here Khitruk seems to refer to an inarticulable quality that each film needs to have in order to evoke in the audience a sense of recognition of the represented reality on a more intimate level. In this film, there is a feeling that the drawings, once taken out of their static nature and put in motion, given a soul, still refuse to spring to life. They only appear as a forced attempt. A different effect was achieved in the following film with the protagonist *Icarus*, who, in his simplicity, exudes a life force and determination that makes him the most active hero among those considered in this chapter.

ICARUS AND THE WISEMEN (IKAR I MUDRETSY, 1976)

In *Icarus and the Wisemen*, Khitruk turns to the Greek myth of Icarus with a twist. In mythology Icarus's flight toward the sun is seen as an act of foolishness, disobedience, and hubris, while in the film, seemingly unwise flights are driven by a determination to follow a dream despite the obstacles posed by a stifling society.

An approach to myths as a basis for reflection on the present emerges in a trend of animation that flourishes in the 1970s. In this tendency, as Krivulia notes, the myth is revised to express an idea that is still valid in present time, and in the process the film acquires multiple interpretative layers; the spectators' interpretation depends on the codes that they have at their disposal, their background, and their cultural experience.[28]

In this film, the myth is rewritten to present a story of a single man with an obsession for flying. The new Icarus links the "little man" of the Russian literary tradition, detached from the rest of society, to the non-conformist artist in a Soviet culture dominated by dogma and doctrines. Ultimately, the film expands beyond the character to a generalized conception of freedom of expression.

Icarus and the Flight

The theme of flight borrowed from the myth is a motif that often recurs in the films of the 1960s. The flight expressed achievements in the cosmos and a consequent sense of superiority and national pride, as well as a movement from a questionable past into a promising future.[29] In the following decade, the 1970s, flight into space is replaced by a more philosophical attitude, filled with subtle political overtone, *Icarus* is such an example.

In the film, the theme becomes more allegorical, personal, and intimate than in previous years. The character's appearance accurately suits this idea, he is no more the muscular, fit, and strong hero or cosmonaut, but instead a simple and funny little man following a personal dream, a foolish person, possessed by a fervent desire to fly.[30] This passion is so intense that it drives him to insane attempts and repetitive catastrophes, but no failure discourages him.[31] The more Icarus tries, the quicker the sages interrupt his flight and attack him with maxims that materialize in the air. Icarus's desire to be different and fly free will soon be utterly crushed by their intervention. The action unfolds through alternating points of view from Icarus to the wisemen and vice versa. Although the sages' mottos provoke his fall, they also seem to be inspired by Icarus's foolish deeds.

The film opens with a classical image of Icarus, a slightly caricatured reproduction in the style of antique Greek painted vases or relief carved in stone. The picture aims to present the defeated Icarus as beautiful and tragic as he is portrayed in myths.[32] Soon after, though, this image gives way to the Icarus in the film, a small and ridiculous person, who, Khitruk says,

> does not in any way resemble a mythical hero. A cap of matted hair, a thin beard, a surprised open mouth and especially those eyes, squinting in different directions (as if looking somewhere past), give him a strange and comical look[33] (Figure 4.8).

The character's first appearance presents him far from the solemn image that is usually associated with the traditional representation of the myth. The effect is to bring the hero down to earth, more like a Chaplinesque figure, in order to evoke the audience's empathy.

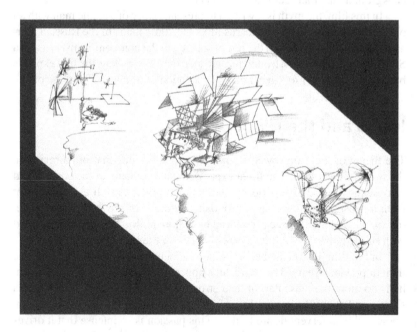

FIGURE 4.8 *Icarus*. Flying Apparatus. Sketch. © Soyuzmultfilm.

His face is first portrayed at the very bottom of the film frame, his eyes fixed on the birds flying. The frame is purposely cutting off most of the character, as if to suggest he will be complete only in his union with the sky, which is, at the same time, a space where he can test his dreams and a symbol of a higher aspiration. Whereas the birds symbolize his dream and his striving for freedom, the more he resembles a bird, the more ridiculous he appears to the spectators' rational minds and their general assumption of the unattainability of such dreams.

His pensive and bewildered expression, his funny gestures and his clumsiness are all traits that recall another creation of Khitruk, Nazarov and Zuikov, *Vinni Pukh*. At one point, Icarus gets entangled in the broken wings, a prisoner of his own creation; another time, he unsticks pieces of wood tangled around his head in the same way as *Vinni Pukh* unplugs the thorns from his nose. His perennially on-the-move figure highly contrasts the sages' dignified poses and motionlessness. Indeed, his deeds appear as an act of rebellion against the static passiveness of the wisemen, which provide an indirect comment on the Soviet period, the Brezhnev's stagnation, during which the film was made.

If Icarus's comic flight attempts are endued with a fast rhythm, the wise men provide a picture of lazy, inactive enjoyment, the same "dolce vita," in which ancient romans are often portrayed. As the script suggests, "it is evident that complacent elders are satisfied with life."[34] They are not stirred by Icarus' feats, they barely move and follow Icarus's fall with their eyes, and then return to their statue-like poses (Figure 4.9).

The alternating images of these two sides, wisemen vs. Icarus, also serves the rhythm of the film, which gets more and more intense by means of a careful edit of the episodes, which progressively reduces the length of pauses in between the attempts.

Words as Weapons

The rhythm of the film is also created by the appearance of words, which concretize in the air with dynamic movements and an energy the wisemen lack. Words are personalized, they move as though they have a life of their own, and they act directly on the character. They are fragmented in single letters and thrown into little clouds without an order. Only then do they reorganize into full words in arrangements that recall the experiments of the early 20th century avant-garde, in which the imagery created by the words in print and the sense of the poems were inextricably connected. As soon as the words take shape, they transform into oppressing means, their semantic value acquires a physical weight. Words come out of the mouths of the sages with ominous sounds and

FIGURE 4.9 *Icarus*. Icarus and the Wisemen. Sketch. © Soyuzmultfilm.

grow in power and weight in multiple senses: they freeze inscribed in stone and turn into increasingly big monuments which literally crash Icarus's dreams.

But Icarus does not despair, he keeps on ascending the cliff at progressively higher speed, with more and more absurd apparatus (from a complicated construction made of levers and slings that recalls Leonardo's sketches to a kite-like apparatus or a paper airplane). One last time, Icarus runs up with

> two wings on the buttocks, a small umbrella between the shoulder blades and a stabilizer on the head, giving him the resemblance to a Roman legionnaire. And in the hands is the steering wheel, which is not connected to anything and therefore absolutely useless.[35]

And here is when the miracle comes into play, he lifts in the sky – the rhythm changes, becoming slow, music echoes for the first time, and the frame fills in with bright colors. Icarus flies, free in the air, ecstatically making all kinds of turns and pirouettes, a simulated close-up shows a blissful smile on his face[36] (Figure 4.10).

Only at this point, when they feel under attack, do the sages move around, scattering in panic. Not for long, as they soon reunite and send up a series of aphorisms in the form of cannon firings, which envelope the flying Icarus until he is completely swamped. A block no longer made of white marble but instead of ominously black granite encloses Icarus, who drops to the ground.

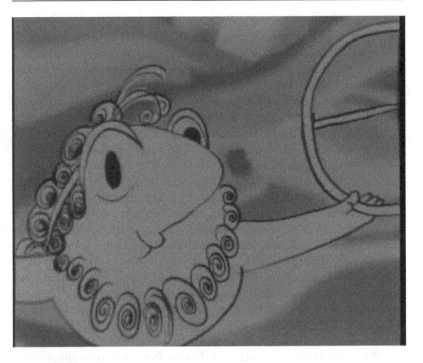

FIGURE 4.10 *Icarus*. Icarus's flight. © Soyuzmultfilm.

A pedestal is there to receive the obelisk, as though this end for Icarus was long awaited, his destiny already predetermined from the very beginning. At this point, the camera zooms out to show the size of this monument among the other little white ones with other dicta inspired by Icarus's previous foolish attempts. Here, the wisemen that caused his fall hypocritically cry over his grave, in the same way as the bureaucrat sheds tears in *Man in the Frame*, or the oppressive Hand mourns the deceased artist in Jiří Trnka's *The Hand*. On the monument, Icarus appears as the tall, elegant, and tragic hero seen at the beginning; the words "non moventur" engraved underneath his image seals the final cessation of movement, the win of stagnation. The aphorisms' final act results in a cemetery of words, the ultimate inertia.

Epilogue

After a brief pause, the film switches to the wisemen visiting the same cemetery of wisdom with their pupils. There is only one boy, who does not follow the herd of cloned students. He looks different from the others, his nose is tiny, he wears glasses that make his eyes bigger, his hair is scruffier, and his look is curious and distracted. While his schoolmates repeat fast and loud the sages' mottos, he notices some feathers scattered on the floor. Next, his tiny figure, detached from the group, appears in the distance with a fantastic structure of feathers and planks on his back, rushing uncontrollably to the top, accompanied by Icarus's music theme (Figure 4.11).

As this new Icarus takes off, the colors invade the sky again as they did for Icarus earlier, but the boy's flight is stopped in mid-air and the title "End of the Film" appears on the screen. We do not see the outcome of the flight, only the music resounds through the title. The director leaves an open end, as though to underline the cyclicality of the events. There will always be Icaruses that step outside of the mass and seek to follow their own individual dreams; and ultimately, their deeds become the very source of inspiration for others.

As happened with *The Man in the Frame*, Khitruk was compelled to create an uplifting ending. The original idea was to conclude the film with the inscription on a piece of marble in the cemetery of wisdom. In the modified ending with a new Icarus, the tragic thought of the film gets lost.[37] Again the director regretted the changes, believing that in both cases the original idea was much deeper than the enforced positive end.[38] Khitruk's original idea was based on the complexity of the character, sweet and funny, but also tragic, as in Akakii Akakievich of Gogol's *The Overcoat*.[39] Both characters are fully immersed in their passion, which is their sole reason to live, but both meet tragic ends.

Political references are evident in the film, from hints to Brezhnev's stagnation to the urge of the artist to break out of the controlled authoritarian dictum over the art, especially in a Soviet society ruled by socialist realism for many years. But in his biography, Khitruk rarely mentions the specific situation of the artist in the Soviet Union, he rather focuses on universal truths and generalized experiences. It is as though Khitruk refuses to engage in a political or overtly dissident discourse, but his resistance to limitation of freedom – wherever it would be – resurfaces in his films.

Khitruk's films expose his urge to break away from conventions, not a rare trait in a master artist, and his desire to make this possible despite the restrictions with which one may be surrounded. This was possible only by reaching a compromise and learning how to navigate the specific society in which he lived. Yet, for Khitruk, the defense of freedom of expression was a topic that went beyond the limits of the socio-political context in which he lived, and it became a universal need, a necessary step in the progress of humanity.

The film is not strictly political, rather it is a philosophical meditation on the themes of freedom, creativity, and determination to reach one's own goals and dreams, despite the attacks from a conformist society. It is also an appeal to recognize the importance of non-complying behavior for the progress of society.

FIGURE 4.11 *Icarus*. New Icarus. Sketch. © Soyuzmultfilm.

A political and at the same time philosophical overtone is present in several Eastern European films, two of which seem to be particularly influential for Khitruk: the already mentioned *The Hand* (*Ruka*, 1965) by Jiří Trnka and another ex-Czechoslovakian film *A Badly Painted Hen* by Jiří Brdečka

(Špatně namalovaná slepice, 1963). While the first one directly tackles the position of the artist in an authoritarian society, the second exalts the right to be different and unique. Khitruk's film combines in itself both aspects.

As Khitruk points out, this film was born in the genre of "film-parable," which has its own rules, of which the most important is laconism.[40] Indeed, the director and his team created a film stripped of unnecessary elements, bare of detailed background, and armed with a simple line drawing, like a caricature, on a white background. Most of the film is in black and white and lacks music; only at the climax, a rainbow of colors fills the screen accompanied by a triumphant soundtrack. The sudden appearance of colors and music in the moment when the protagonist begins to fly is certainly effective; however, the overall film perhaps might appear too bare to fully engage the spectators. In the following films, Khitruk delves deeper into visual experimentation, elaborating in an original way static material, such as Engels's letters and sketches (*The Young Friedrich Engels*, 1970), works from the fine arts (*A Day Before Our Era*, 1977) and reproduction of ancient Greek art (*Olympics*, 1982).

NOTES

1   Beumers, "Comforting Creatures in Children's Cartoons," 154.
2   Nikitkina, "Sotsial'no-nravstvennaia problematika i novyi geroi v sovetskoi mul'tiplikatsii 70–80-x godov," 62–64. Anti-war films appeared in these years in poster-like form or in caricature style reminiscent of the first animation films of the 1920s (*Peace to Your House*, 1962; *It is in Our Power*, 1970), or in a mixture of styles and a strong propagandistic stance (*Ave Maria*, Ivanov-Vano, Danilevich, 1972).
3   Including the Annecy film festival in 1965 and in Mamaia in 1966, which seems to have an important impact on him. Khitruk, "Sto vosem' vstrech."
4   See meeting with East-German animators about the question of politics in films, whose minutes are recorded in *Politicheskaia tema v mul'tiplikatsionnom kino*.
5   *Politicheskaia tema v mul'tiplikatsionnom kino*, 16–17.
6   *Politicheskaia tema v mul'tiplikatsionnom kino*, 16.
7   Norstein, "On vnes inoe ponimanie izobrazheniia...," 247.
8   A film made in 1967 by the director Lev Atamanov, *The Bench* (*Skameika*), borrowed the idea of the bench as a center of the action for the entire film. In this film, based on sketches by the Dutch caricaturist Herluf Bidstrup, it is not one protagonist but the bench itself that remains static at the center of the screen. As in Dovniković's *Curiosity* and Khitruk's *The Island*, in this film visitors succeed each other, showcasing mini-sketches of different personalities and social classes.

9 The hero in *The Island* not only reminds one of the aforementioned character in Zaniković's film, but also, in his simple traits and nakedness, he recalls the main character in Popescu-Gopo's films.

10 Nazarov, "Edik! Est' neplokhaia ideia...," 283. Borodin reports details in the approval process of the film *The Wild West* in Borodin, "Animatsiia podnevol'naia," n.d. Chapter 4, 29–30.

11 This scene caused much discussion within the team, as Khitruk wanted the statue of the *David,* while Zuikov thought of a statue of Buddha (deep in meditation – not noticing being moved), in the end they agreed on Michelangelo's "dormant" Dying Slave. Khitruk and Asenin, "Kuda idet mul'tiplikatsiia," 66.

12 Khitruk, *Professiia-animator*, 2007, 1: 199.

13 Khitruk, 1: 199.

14 This anecdote is told by Khitruk on a few occasions – Khitruk, 1: 199–201, as well as by Norstein in Norstein, "Priznanie masteru," 300.

15 For a discussion on a multi-faceted process in the creation of an animated film, see Prokhorov, Anatolii "Èvolutsiia animatografa: ot mul'tiplikatsii k 'fantomu svobody,'" 38–39.

16 Khitruk, *Professiia-animator*, 2007, 1: 260.

17 Venzher, *Sotvorenie fil'ma*, 125.

18 Venzher, 126.

19 Venzher, 126.

20 Venzher, 126.

21 Khitruk, *Professiia-animator*, 2007, 1: 299.

22 Venzher, *Sotvorenie fil'ma*, 126.

23 Piretto, *Quando c'era l'URSS. 70 anni di storia culturale sovietica*, 71–72.

24 For a discussion on the topic, see Reid, "The Khrushchev Kitchen: Domesticating the Scientific-Technological Revolution."

25 Boym, *Common Places: Mythologies of Everyday Life in Russia*, 255.

26 Maliukova, "Poteriav, ne chuvstvoval sebia poteriannym."

27 Epstein, "For a New Avant-Garde," 352.

28 Krivulia, *Labirinty animatsii*, 78–84.

29 For a brief discussion of films related to the cosmos, see Pontieri, *Soviet Animation and the Thaw*, 57–58.

30 Khitruk, *Professiia-animator*, 2007, 1: 175.

31 Khitruk, 1: 177.

32 Khitruk, 1: 236.

33 Khitruk, 1: 237.

34 Khitruk, 1: 238.

35 Khitruk, 1: 246.

36 Khitruk, 1: 246.

37 Khitruk, 1: 180–181.

38 Khitruk, 1: 181.

39 Khitruk, 1: 181.

40 Volkov, "Razgovor o professii," 186.

In Search for Unconventional Sources

The Young Friedrich Engels (1970), *A Day Before Our Era* (1977), and *Olympics* (1982)

Khitruk strived to find the best visual solution for the issue at hand in each of his movies, but there are three films in particular in which he attempted to employ more unconventional material. At the end of the 1960s, he animated sketches and drawings made by a young Friedrich Engels, as well as engravings and pictures of his era; in the late 1970s, together with Iurii Norstein, he employed works from the fine arts in *A Day Before Our Era*; and in the early 1980s, he reproduced ancient Greek art in *Olympics*. For each of these films, texts from different realms were taken from their original source and animated, resulting in unique experiments.

DOI: 10.1201/9781003199625-6

THE YOUNG FRIEDRICH ENGELS (IUNOSHA FRIDRIK ENGELS, 1970)

At the end of the 1960s, a delegation from the German Democratic Republic, including the head of the Dresden animation studio DEFA Wolfgang Kernik and the director Katia Georgi, visited Soyuzmultfilm and invited Khitruk and Vadim Kurchevskii to work together on a film about Friedrich Engels to celebrate the 150th anniversary of his birth. Khitruk's first reaction was bewilderment "I was brave, but not so brave as to imagine that animation can make a film about the classics of Marxism."[1] The idea, though, was to make a film on the young Engels before his work with Marx. Kernik showed them the letters, drawings, and caricatures a youthful Engels sent to his relatives. Khitruk was fascinated by this talented young man, who composed music, knew many languages, and wrote poetry, literary, and political articles at a young age.[2]

Khitruk and Kurchevskii accepted the challenge and joined the directors Katia and Claus Georgi at the German studio. The film was the first co-production of the Soviet studio Soyuzmultfilm and the East-German DEFA Studio für Trickfilme.[3] The directors did not want to make a political film about Marxism-Leninism, rather a film about "an eccentric young man unusually gifted."[4] Yet, this approach was a risky undertaking, and it was approved with some hesitation. Norstein mentions that the film caused some stir at Goskino,[5] and doubtless the authorities looked with apprehension at the treatment of the canonic ideological figure in a humanized way, with weaknesses and troubles of his young age.[6]

The script was finalized in December 1969, under the endorsement of a specialist of the Institute of Marxism-Leninism of the Central Committee of the CPSU[7] and the control of Goskino, which suggested a few cuts and, in particular, a recommendation to "carefully consider the visual range of the film, specifically, the image of F. Engels on the screen."[8]

When talking about the film, Khitruk does not focus on the obvious risks on the political ground, i.e., the need to produce a politically sound film that would exalt the figure of the future political theoretician and revolutionary; instead, he openly expresses his fear that a failure in this endeavor would prevent artists from experimenting with unconventional methods in the future.[9]

The project certainly offered a stimulating and enriching experience, but it required an innovative approach to unusual material, which posed some challenges for the realization of a whole film,

> We wrote the script in this way: we got the letters, laid them down and thought about the order we would use them and how to find a key that would allow us to go from one letter to the other, from one caricature to the other.[10]

The work was complex at any stage, but the ending presented an additional challenge. Only did Kernik's passing suggestion to end the film at the very beginning of Engels's collaboration with Marx take them out of the impasse; after all, they thought, the rest of Engels' life was already familiar to the spectators,[11] especially if raised in a communist country.

The film covers only four years of the life of Engels, from 1838 to 1842, during most of which Engels lived in Bremen while undertaking a business apprenticeship at an export firm under the insistence of his father. In letters to his friends and mostly to his sister, Engels revealed in words and in drawings an image of "his excitable youthful nature,"[12] along with a condemning picture of Bremen's frivolous society.

The letters are organized in a way in which serious speculations about religion and political ideas are intermingled with facetious comments about haircuts, moustaches, fashion, or the *Listzomania* that spread around the composer at that time. Engels was an active participant of Bremen's social life, but he also placed himself above those around him, whom he accused of being trivial dandies or boring chatterboxes. In his letter to his sister, he boasted of his achievements not only as an intellectual, but also as a strong active man, versed in horseback riding, swimming, and fencing. His letters are filled with a youthful joking spirit, as when he mentions his moustache style is not gladly accepted in society but liked by the ladies; or how he wore his shiny buttons at a poet's reading, making the lecturer lose his thread of thoughts; or when he talks about teaching his dog the command "That's an aristocrat," to trigger a growl.

His extravagant behavior shocked Bremen society, as did his harsh political pamphlets – like the one in which he condemns landlords for resorting to children labor and then easily appeasing their conscience through pious religious practices. The film repetitively shows Engels's political ideas interweaved with less serious topics; for example, he comments on his singing and composing soon after a sequence in which he admonishes a series of monarchs to watch for the powerful strength of the "union of the young people."

The alternating moods convey the directors' desire to present an image of Engels that expresses his young age, his temperament, and his language full of irony and humor. On the other hand, the spontaneous comments on multiple facets of society illustrate how the formation of Engels's political and revolutionary ideas developed at a young age and stemmed from his perceptive nature.

FIGURE 5.1   *Engels*. Engels at the desk surrounded by characters. © Soyuzmultfilm.

The depiction of Engels' life in Bremen ends with a frame that gathers all caricatures and drawings seen so far. All characters come forth for a last call, arranged on the screen around Engel seated at his desk (a recurring image throughout the film) (Figure 5.1).

An era in his life comes to an end; the following sequence shows Engels departing to Berlin in 1841 to serve in the army, where he has a chance to audit Berlin University, the "arena of intellectual battles," and "contemporary thoughts."[13] From here, in 1842, Engels leaves for Manchester, where a new phase of his life begins. Drawings are now substituted by engravings and pictures of the rising proletariat. The film finishes with these last words "In the struggling of the proletariat, he recognized the only force that solely was capable of changing the world." The last frame is a blank page, on which a now familiar calligraphy writes "Dear Marx." The rest is known history.

Animated Drawings, Caricatures, and Words

Engels's letters are complemented with drawings that offer a visual accompaniment to the words. Letters, drawings, caricatures, and sketches of the young Engels appear on the screen in the making, brought to life trait by trait with a technique that goes back to the early stages of animation, when artists would quickly draw on the board their characters in so-called *lightning sketches*. The technique provides a sense of immediacy and strongly links the strokes with their author. Engels's drawings are faithfully presented with a neutral background so as to underline the paper on which they were sketched and emphasize once more their authorship. The lines of the manuscript text are scribbled on an invisible flat paper sheet to accentuate the flatness of the screen and so foreground the link between the cinematic medium and Engels's written text.[14]

The words from Engels's letters materialize in concert with the voice of the narrator, the actor Viktor Tatarskii, who presents Engels's point of view in first person. The off-screen voice, on the one hand, further underlines the authorship of the film, and on the other, as Zakrzhevskaia notices, "being in tune with the image, counterpointing or merging with it, it 'cements' the action and ensures the integrity of aesthetic perception."[15] The effect is a tight unity of spoken words, written words, and images, which erase the line that demarcates each of them, presenting an image of the young Engels that is inextricably linked with his own ideas and words.

The fact that the film is based on letters and drawings by Engels makes him not only the character but also the author of the film. This device gives credibility to the film and protects the directors from the accusation of deviating from the canonical view of the father of communism. The choice of such an important figure also gives animation a more serious status, raising it to a form of art that goes beyond childish entertainment, but becomes a meeting point of various art forms, from visual art to poetry and music.

A film such as *The Young Fredrick Engels* also brings animation closer to the cinematic documentary genre. However, paradoxically, the more the film aims to a documentary status, the more it employs a conventionalized language. Background is manipulated as stage decoration, flat marionettes representing members of Bremen society act as though in a puppet theater, putting on a superficial show directed by the invisible strings of societal conventions.

Cut-outs of figures from journals of the time become characters in the film, a device that emphasizes the superficiality and flatness of their personality. The journal cut-outs and illustrations are organized on a flat surface in the form of a collage, in which the original source maintains its properties and "historicity" while at the same time appears in a new context, provoking a rearrangement with a hint of irony.

Engels, instead, is usually represented with simple sketch-lines on a sepia background. The only times that his figure takes the form of a flat marionette is when he is serving in the army, a time where his free spirit is confined by inevitable ties. Most of the time, the directors represent Engels as detached from Bremen society, often resorting to a split screen, wherein the screen is divided into sections, in two halves or in a triptych, with Engels filling one side physically separated from the rest of society. In one such triptych he appears with a cigar in his mouth, ready to literally blow the interlocutors out with a puff of his cigar (Figure 5.2).

FIGURE 5.2 *Engels*. Triptych with Engels in the middle. © Soyuzmultfilm.

Engel's Thought through Music, Sound, and Images

Music and sound add another layer in the film. The expressive non-diegetic music composed by Wolfgang Pietsch appropriately underlines the shifts of mood throughout the film. At one point, the soundtrack gives way to the choral composed by Engels himself. This shift from non-diegetic soundtrack to diegetic music emphasizes the dramatic play built around Engels being at the same time the object and subject of the film, character and off-screen author.

The sound and music accompany the images in a way that goes beyond the traditional association. In a specific scene, religious images appear to the sound of church bells, zooming in and out, mimicking the movement of the bell. Here, sound and image forcibly fill the frame, as if to emphasize Engels's diatribe against the imposing force used by religion to restrain an individual's freedom.

Engels's intransigence toward any limitation on his "spirit of freedom" (by religion or societal constrictions alike) becomes more and more pronounced with the unraveling of the film. The manifestation of his conviction is reflected in the visual choices adopted by the directors.

At the beginning, Engel's drawings offer "documentary evidence" of the unfolding of his thoughts and serves as commentary to his humorous words.[16] But once the discourse shifts to serious problems, such as workers conditions and child labor, cut-outs and drawings are substituted by engravings and real photographs, which express the mood and provide a direct reference to a reality that deeply concerned Engels. At this point in the film, as in his life, his words represent more intensively his urge to move into the socio-political sphere. He dismisses his earlier articles on literary or philosophical matters for the Jahrbücher as an exercise, merely experiments to understand whether he would be able to "participate actively in the movement of the century." The need to formulate his ideas in a written form will result in *The Communist Manifesto* and his work on Marx's *The Capital*. The film stops at this very conjunction.

A DAY BEFORE OUR ERA (ZA DEN' NASHEGO ERY. FRAGMENT, 1977. UNRELEASED)

Seven years passed from the release of the film on Engels before Khitruk embarked again in experiments with pre-existent visual material. This time, Khitruk, together with Iurii Norstein,[17] drew upon images from famous artists' artworks in a film meant to celebrate the 60th anniversary of the Revolution. Only a five-minute fragment attests to the remarkable creative process behind it; the film was never completed. After getting acquainted with the historical material, the directors realized that the theme could not be developed in the way they originally thought; it would only end up depicting tragedy, something that they did not desire, neither would be allowed.[18] Indeed, once the fragment was completed and shown publicly at the Museum of Cinema in Moscow, it struck the audience for being counter-revolutionary rather than celebrating the anniversary of the Revolution. The authors were probably safe only because the video was not intended for distribution and the censorship did not pay attention to it.[19] The experimental short was not released and the directors decided to suspend the work. As Borodin points out, the footage, once taken out of the context of the French Revolution, refuses this context itself, and reflects the directors' real attitude toward the subject.[20] The experiment was almost forgotten until 2012, when it was screened among other archival material at Belye Stolby Festival, and later at Dom Kino.[21]

Animating Works of Art

The film reflects Khitruk and Norstein's fascination with the use of static material in animation, which both directors expressed in previous films:

Khitruk with the employment of photographs in *Man in the Frame* and *Film, Film, Film*; Norstein with works of revolutionary artists in his first film about the revolution, *25th First Day* (*25-oe pervyi den'*, Norstein, Tiurin, 1968), or fresco, ancient miniatures and icons in *The Siege of Kerzhenets* (*Secha pri Kerzhentse*, Norstein, Ivanov-Vano, 1971). Incidentally, a few other animated films made during the 1960s and 1970s utilized classic artworks, among the most significant experiments are Khrzhanovskii's use of classical masterpieces in *The Glass Harmonica* (1968), and the Ukrainian Nina Vasilenko's animated icons in her *The Tale of Igor's Campaign* (*Skazannia pro Igoriv pokhid/Skazanie pro Igorev pokhod*, 1972, Kyivnaukfilm/Kievnauchfil'm).[22]

In *A Day Before Our Era*, both directors take their early experiments to the extreme in a search for a kind of animation that transcends its traditional understanding. The title of the surviving fragment sounds more like a headline for an experiment report than a film: "Elaboration of the method of animation and technology for filming finished works of fine art in animated films."

The two directors juxtapose pictures of static material in a way that creates a movement or a reaction that is only hinted at in the figures. Using static images in a frame-by-frame approach is typical of animation, yet this is an unusual undertaking. The emphasis is not on the movement but on the static images that come to life without morphing the lines in the picture itself. The raw material is used as it is, adding only "external" effects. The two artists go beyond traditional animation and suggest new canons, which are entirely defined by light, composition, editing, rhythm, and camera movement. These are devices that had been used in previous films, but here they are handled to substitute almost completely traditional character movements and dominate the entire project. The images are explored from different angles and camera distance in order to create a story. It is the dynamic quality intrinsic in the images that is exploited.

It is curious that a skilled animator like Khitruk – who could create seamless movements in his characters like no one else – once he became a director, was rather fascinated by those static images that could reveal the essence of movements in themselves. With this film, it is no more the process of the movement that is important for him, but the key points in the process. As Norstein explains, discreteness of movement affects the audience more vividly, "the distance between key-drawings is not felt like a physical movement, but like an action that develops in your consciousness."[23] The spectators are left to fill in the gaps subconsciously and in doing so, they begin to follow what takes place inside the characters, instead of the mere action, and perceive more intensely the theme of the film.[24]

The original design for the film was to have a split screen (a recurrent device in Khitruk's films) like a triptych: in the center, the depiction of the various phases of the October Revolution, in particular the events between October 24 and October 26, 1917; on the sides, images of historical uprisings preceding the Russian upheaval. The directors aimed to provide a visual and historical background for the October events, making of the Russian Revolution the natural historical result and the starting point of a new era.[25]

Music as a Layer in the Structure

While the images convey the story and provide a hermeneutic key to the events, the music offers an additional interpretative layer. Norstein suggested they include in the film Dmitrii Shostakovich's Fifth Symphony. It seemed to him that the music, with its combination of harmony and imperious sounds, could express the "transition into inexpressible tragedy," "the drama of power."[26] As already visible in his earlier works, Norstein was particularly interested in the ways the visual image could be juxtaposed with the music creating harmony and contrast. In the film *The Seasons* (*Vremena goda*, 1969), the three-dimensional figures inspired by the style of Viatska toys move through traditional folkloric decorations at the rhythm of Tchaikovsky's cycle "The seasons;" or, even more influential for *The Day Before Our Era*, is *The Battle of Kerzhenets* (*Secha pri Kerzhentse*, 1971), in which icons, Russian frescoes and miniatures of the XIV–XV centuries were animated according to the music of the symphonic interlude of Rimsky-Korsakov's opera *The Legend of the Invisible City of Kitezh* (*Skazanie o nevidimom grade Kitezhe i deve Fevronni*).[27]

Likewise, in *A Day Before Our Era*, Shostakovich's symphony constituted a layer in the montage structure.[28] With hindsight, Norstein notices that the juxtaposition of the images and music did not always provide the dynamism necessary to convey the mood or the essence of the revolution. In particular, he points out the scene of the Oath at Versailles. Here, according to Norstein, the montage was "not sharp enough." While Jacque-Louis David's unfinished fresco "Royal Tennis Court Oath at Versailles" expressed the people's euphoria, Shostakovich's music and the rhythm created by the montage did not fully convey the atmosphere, instead it dragged the mood; a mistake they could not correct at that time[29] (Figure 5.3).

From that scene of rejoicing and celebration of freedom, though, the tragedy of the struggle for power begins. The change of mood, Norstein says, resonates in "the wheezing of the horns in a lower register" which "literally materialized a new monstrous power."[30]

FIGURE 5.3 *A Day Before Our Era*. Scene based on Jacque-Louis David's "Royal Tennis Court Oath at Versailles." © Soyuzmultfilm.

The Two Faces of Revolutions

Even though the film script focused on the October Revolution, the objective was to go beyond its mere celebration and explore the implications of revolutionary events. Norstein explains,

> The main idea came down to the fact that there is power, there are people, and when the proportions between power and people are violated, when people are crushed to the limit, physically and morally, they explode – like a clogged cauldron. The people sweep away the power, a new one comes, and the people again find themselves under this power.[31]

This is the theme of the film, and a thought, Norstein adds, that often recurs in Khitruk's works.

The shooting of the short film occurred in parallel with the collection and research of the material.[32] The plan was to begin with an episode about the French Revolution, seen as the predecessor to the Russian Revolution and as an example of the strong power inherent in the people's will. The directors did not necessarily choose material that was historically linked with a specific revolution, rather they selected the visual images and music that would convey the idea of power, of revolution with its unleashed exultation as well as the dire consequences. According to the script, the film was supposed to be based on the works of famous artists, namely, Dürer, Gericault, Daumier, Jacques-Louis David, Bruegel, and Bosch.[33]

The episode depicted in the fragment opens with Andrea del Verrocchio's equestrian statue "Condottiero Colleoni" (Figure 5.4) followed by Pieter Bruegel the Elder's *The Blind Leading the Blind* (Figure 5.5).

The juxtaposition of these two works forms a structural frame for the short film and provides a comment on the relation between power and the people's condition. The statue, striking for its intrinsic dynamism, is brought to life by an effective composition of the frame, low camera angles, and montage of images and music. The scene strongly recalls Eisenstein's and Pudovkin's montage with footage of similar monuments and achieves an analogous effect of strength, energy, and overpowering force.

The composition of Bruegel's painting, presented in discrete units and as a whole with a strong dynamic effect, represents the eternal fate of people following rulers who, instead of moving them forward, lead them astray. It is significant that in the film the directors do not reproduce the fallen blind who guides the others as in the original painting. This creates the effect of having the Condottiero Colleoni become the commander of the blind men. At the same time, by not showing the leading blind's fall, which stops their path, the directors underline the cyclical nature of historical events.

FIGURE 5.4 *A Day Before Our Era*. Scene based on Verrocchio's "Condottiero Colleoni." © Soyuzmultfilm.

FIGURE 5.5 *A Day Before Our Era.* Scene based on Bruegel's *The Blind Leading the Blind.* © Soyuzmultfilm.

The elaboration of various famous works of art gives the opportunity to look at the idea of revolution from a variety of points of views, from the perspective of the author of the work of art to the directors' reinterpretation through their montage. The fusion of the two perspectives creates a complex vision of reality that eschews a unilateral interpretation of revolutionary events. Besides, the reality so formed brings together past, present and future, turning the historical events into a timeless generalized reflection of human nature and historical cycles.

The directors approached the revolution from both sides: the heroic acts of those who believed in a better future and freedom, and what inevitably came afterwards. As Norstein explains,

> I looked at these figures, at those who really gave their lives for the future, for a different attitude towards the world, for a different air, and I treated them, of course, as heroes who sacrificed themselves for the future good. This is a completely natural attitude, dictated simply by their actions. We see a lot of this in the revolution. Yes, indeed, blood, shooting – it was all because it was a tectonic shift.

But there is another side, says Norstein,

> a new government comes, it gives some concessions, but it does not care at all about how the lower classes live [...] the leaders of the revolution,

with all their humanitarian intentions, with all their promises, while they consider their own truth to be more truthful than the truth of another, they immediately turn into that evil force that, in the end, devours itself.[34]

In the film, the result of this destroying force is effectively expressed in the reproduction of Goya's engravings of the cycle "The Disaster of War." *A Day Before Our Era*, though, does not end with a catastrophic image, it also calls for a more righteous solution. Toward the end, there is an image of the open sky above all these events that constitutes a third level in the film, it represents, Norstein says, "the air that people should breathe; and this applies not only to the revolution, but also to the present day."[35]

This idea of cyclicality, yet with a glimpse of hope, returns in another of Khitruk's films, *Olympics* (*Olimpioniki*, 1982), made later, in 1982, with the collaboration of Norstein as animator. In this film about the history of the Olympics, instead of the tragedy of the war, Khitruk chooses the path of celebrating peace.

OLYMPICS (OLIMPIONIKI, 1982)

Olympics presents a brief story of the Greek Olympic Games from its origin to the present. In this film, Khitruk opts for various techniques: experimental footage introduces the theme, characters drawn from Greek vases and marble statues present the birth of the tradition, and then, live-action footage and photographs display its evolution in modern days.

The choice of the theme for this film was not fortuitous; the Olympic Games in Moscow in 1980 gave rise to several films on the subject, from films with the Olympic Bear Mascot to a cycle of one to three-minute micro-films under the name of "Olympics 1980" ("Olimpiada -80", Mul'ttelefil'm). The Olympic theme was also adopted in famous series such as Volodymyr Dakhno's *Cossacks* (*Kozaki*, and specifically, *How the Cossacks become Olympians, Iak kozaki olimpiitsiami stali/ Kak kazaki olimpiitsami stali*, 1978) at the Ukrainian Studio Kyivnaukfilm (known in Soviet time also as Kievnauchfil'm) and, although only peripherally, Kotenochkin's series *Just you Wait! Episode 13* (*Nu pogodi! 13*).[36] Closer to the spirit of Khitruk's film were two short animated films on the history of the ancient Greek Olympiad. The first, *The Wheel of Fortune* (*Koleso fortuny*, Solin, 1980, Ekran), presents the story in a cartoonish style close to Jean Effel's caricatures. The second, *The Great Relay* (*Bol'shaia estafeta*, Aksenchuk, 1979), begins with images drawn from an ancient vase's painting and elaborates the origin of the

Olympic Games in a style similar to the one then adopted by Khitruk's team (although, the film, further develops in a poster-style manner).

The material employed in Khitruk's short was initially prepared for a drawn-animation insert for a documentary film about the Moscow 1980 Olympic Games, *Oh Sport, You are Peace!* (*O sport – ty mir!* Iurii Ozerov, 1981). Many of the scenes they prepared did not find a place in the documentary, but once they finished the clip, Khitruk's team decided to expand it and give life to this unused material in an independent animated film.

Opening Sequence

The film begins with a 30-second sequence animated by Norstein. In this introduction, Norstein rearranges images of the bas-reliefs of the Pergamon Altar in a unique frame-by-frame montage of the kind he and Khitruk employed in *A Day Before Our Era*. Discrete units from the bas-relief clash in an accelerated montage of images taken from different angles and various camera distance; flashes of light emphasize the play with shadows and creases intrinsic in the statues and convey a strong chiaroscuro effect. The pulsing of the light and the slight variations of angles create a stereoscopic effect, the statues become wearily alive. Only do synecdochical fragments of the bodies throb forward, showing glimpses of limbs during a heated battle. Increasingly intense music marks the accelerated rhythm of the succession of the images, organized in a montage that draws its teaching from Eisenstein's tradition and achieves a similarly stirring effect. This brief footage aims to portray the victory of Zeus in the mythological battle against the Giants as a way to introduce the legend about the Ancient Olympic Games being originally part of a religious festival in honor of Zeus. After this brief introduction, the style adopted in the film changes. The following scene resorts to Greek vase decorations and ancient statues to illustrate other legends and stories about the origin of the Olympics and its development (Figure 5.6).

Animating Greek Vases' Figures

A narrative voice accompanies the transition from the introductory footage to the faithful reproductions of Greek archaic artworks, which begin to morph into drawn figures. The characters soon become animated, but, in the transition, they lose their solemnity and acquire a cartoonish quality that clashes with the opening sequence.

The characters' traits take shape following the shift in tone, from the serious and dramatic beginning to the elaboration of the story with wit and

FIGURE 5.6   *Olympics*. Storyboard with photos and drawings. © Soyuzmultfilm.

humor. Yet, the cartoonish characters do not shed the stiffness of the static artwork and appear lifeless; in this instance, the concise and laconic style that made Khitruk's films famous clashes with the material available. Even the rhythm, usually Khitruk's strength, seems to drag.

Recycling available material without having a preconception of the work rarely leads to satisfactory results. Khitruk himself was dissatisfied, admitting that the "film was not his subject" and the decision to undertake this project was a little "opportunistic."[37] He was bound by the material that he, together with art directors Vladimir Zuikov and Liudmila Koshkina, already prepared for the documentary film, and only later did he realize that in order to make a good film, it would have been necessary to start all over.[38]

Khitruk is at his best when the material can be animated without constrictions. If the material does not grant this freedom, the spectator has the feeling that the soul of the director is not there, that the material moves without an *anima*. Norstein talks about this risk in animating a work of art in a class recorded in *Animatograficheskie zapiski*, "Any work of art, and a significant work of art in particular, contains compositional completeness. Hence, inviolability! And any animation is a forcible entry into this organism."[39] In order to be able to animate, he explains, a director needs to be drawn by the theme and understand what unites him or her to the artist of the artwork; only at that point would an insight on how to animate the art piece come.[40] This comment reveals the reason why the thirty-second sequence animated by Norstein is the most successful segment of the film, the rest of it was perhaps too distant for Khitruk to reveal a soul.

A Return to Present Time with Photography

At the end of the animated episodes, the film introduces photographs and live-action sequences to draw a link between the ancient tradition and modern time. As with the photographs in *Man in the Frame*, the montage of this final footage exploits the movements inherent in the pictures and gives life, with pan shots and close-ups, to the stills of the athletes in a dynamic way. Photographs and footage of sportsmen in training present a down-to-earth, accessible image of the athletes, while a clip of children performing in synchrony gymnastics choreographies in front of posters exalting physical exercise recalls the Soviet appropriation of the cult of the body. These images give way to a brief succession of short clips of the Moscow Olympics, intercut by shots of a burning Olympic torch, with which the film ends. The torch waits to be passed; the tradition continues.

With the following film, *The Lion and the Bull* (1983), Khitruk passes on the last torch. It is his final film as a director, before turning full time to mentoring and teaching young animators. The theme of his last work becomes more philosophical and expresses a concern for the complexity of the human mind that is present in earlier films, but only in this one is expressed in all its tragedy.

NOTES

1 Khitruk, "O fil'makh. O zarozhdenii idei fil'ma," 54; Khitruk, *Professiia-animator*, 2007, 1: 192.
2 Khitruk, *Professiia-animator*, 2007, 1: 192.
3 Volkov, "Razgovor o professii," 185. Another co-production between communist countries in these years was created for the film *Strange Bird* (*Strannaia ptitsa*, 1969) directed by Zagrebfilm animator Borivoj (Bordo) Dovnikovic with the contribution of Viacheslav Kotenochkin.
4 Khitruk, "O fil'makh. O zarozhdenii idei fil'ma," 65. Khitruk, *Professiia-animator*, 2007, 1: 192.

5 Norstein, "Priznanie masteru," 301. However, there was support inside the studio, see the director Kachanov's comment about being impressed by the attempt to transform a monumental figure into a person. *Politicheskaia tema v mul'tiplikatsionnom kino*, 37.

6 Borodin, "Animatsiia podnevol'naia," n.d. Ch. 4, 24–25.

7 See the specialist N. Belousova's letter with the approval of the script, in "Delo Iunosha Fridrikh Engel's Soiuzmul'tfil'm," 6.

8 "Delo Iunosha Fridrikh Engel's Soiuzmul'tfil'm," 5; Borodin, "Animatsiia podnevol'naia," n.d. Ch. 4, st. 24–25. See also a detailed letter with a list of revisions in "Delo Iunosha Fridrikh Engel's Soiuzmul'tfil'm," 12.

9 Volkov, "Razgovor o professii," 185.

10 Khitruk, *Professiia-animator*, 2007, 1: 198.

11 Khitruk, 1: 198.

12 Asenin, *Volshebniki ekrana. Esteticheskie problemy sovremennoi mul'tiplikatsiia*, 250.

13 Quotation from the film.

14 A similar effect will also be achieved by Khrzhanovskii in his trilogy on Pushkin's works, see a perceptive analysis of the films in Yampolsky, "The Space of Animated Film. Khrzhanovskii's 'I Am with You Again' and Norstein's 'The Tale of Tales,'" 97.

15 Zakrzhevskaia, "Na poroge velikoi zhizni," 79.

16 In a similar way, Pushkin's drawings animated in Khrzhanovskii's later trilogy of films on the Russian bard are closely related to the handwritten page, often offering a commentary on the text, and function, in Mikhail Gurevich's words, as "documentary evidence of the creative process." See more about Khrzhanovskii's Pushkin trilogy, in Gurevich, "Pokadrovoe chtenie: literature i animatsiia," 107.

17 Norstein agreed to participate in the project as co-director and this decision postponed the release of his film *Tale of Tales*. Borodin, "'Za Den' do nashei ery' – zaiavka i istoriia."

18 Borodin; Norstein, "Iurii Norstein o Rabote Nad Fil'mom 'Za Den' Do Nashei Ery.'" As Norstein commented, "And when we began to collect material, we came across so many atrocities of the French Revolution, reflected in the engravings, that I said: 'Fëdor Savel'yevich, we cannot make a film in the form in which it was conceived.' I've never seen any of this before. I knew that heads were flying, it was understandable, but I had no idea – in what quantities! T And when I read that in the month of October alone almost 70,000 heads had been taken ... Then, Khitruk and I had a rather long conversation, I remember, in a vacant lot, behind the 'barn' house. And I said, 'No, I can't make this movie like that, it won't be true. The revolution is a chain of atrocities.'" Borodin, "Animatsiia podnevol'naia," n.d. Ch. 4, 29–30.

19 Borodin, "Animatsiia podnevol'naia," n.d. Ch. 4, 30.

20 Borodin, "'Za Den' do nashei ery' – zaiavka i istoriia."

21 Mikhailin, "Vysshie formy – 'Za den' do nashei ery' Fedora Khitruka i Iuriia Norsteina."

22 Engravings too had been animated, as early as 1932 in Berthold Bartosch's *The Idea* (*L'Idée*, based on engravings by Frans Masereel) and in the Soviet Union in a later film by the Estonian director Rein Raamat, *Hell* (Pôrgu, 1983,

Tallinnfilm, based on Eduard Viiralt's engravings). In the subsequent years, Khrzhanovskii would experiment with animating static material in other films, specifically, elaborating drawings and sketches by Pushkin, Brodsky, Fellini and Sooster.

23 Norstein qtd. in Mikhailin, "Vysshie formy – 'Za den' do nashei ery' Fedora Khitruka i Iuriia Norsteina."
24 Mikhailin.
25 Khitruk, "'Za Den' Do Nashei Ery' – Stsenarnii Plan Mul'tiplikatsionnogo Fil'ma."
26 Norstein, "Iurii Norstein o Rabote Nad Fil'mom 'Za Den' Do Nashei Ery.'"
27 The 1970s saw more examples of films based on famous musical works – see for ex. *The Nutcracker* (Boris Stepantsev, 1973) on Tchaikovsky's music, or *The Songs of Fiery Years* (Inessa Kovalevskaia, 1971) based on popular Civil War songs. Also, on a lighter note, quite a few musicals were released in these years, the most famous probably *Bremen Musicians* (Inessa Kovalevskaia, 1969) and its sequel *On the Trail of the Bremen Town Musicians* (Vasilii Livanov, 1973), or later *The Blue Puppy* (Efim Gamburg, 1976), whose songs were performed by famous singers and actors, such as Alisa Freindlikh, Aleksandr Gradskii, Mikhail Boiarskii, and Andrei Mironov.
28 Norstein, "Iurii Norstein o Rabote Nad Fil'mom 'Za Den' Do Nashei Ery.'"
29 Norstein.
30 Norstein.
31 Norstein.
32 Borodin, "'Za Den' do nashei ery' – zaiavka i istoriia."
33 Boiarsky, *Literaturnye kollazhi*, 150.
34 Norstein, "Iurii Norstein o Rabote Nad Fil'mom 'Za Den' Do Nashei Ery.'"
35 Norstein.
36 See for more details a thorough article on the production of films about the Olympics: Borodin, "Olimpiada pod znakom medvedia."
37 Khitruk, *Professiia-animator*, 2007, 1: 299.
38 Khitruk, 1: 299.
39 Norstein, "Lektsii dlia slushatelei," 29.
40 Norstein, 30.

The Last Torch

6

The Lion and the Bull (1983)

With his last directorial film, Khitruk approaches once more an unusual genre for traditional Soviet animation. This time it was a tale resurfacing from his childhood memory that demanded his attention. The story of *The Lion and the Bull*, an old Eastern parable reminiscent of Shakespearian tragedies, tells how these two strong and powerful animals peacefully living in the same prairie came to fight each other under the influence of an envious and malignant jackal.

The decision to dive into this new adventure is personal – Khitruk recalls how deeply this book affected him in his childhood[1] – but it also occurs at a time when animation was seen to a greater extent as a form of art able to approach a variety of genres. New topical issues were expressed either with irony and parody, or with lyricism. If Khitruk often followed the first tendency, now with his desire to approach eternal and universal philosophical questions, he came closer to that poetic vein that already started at the end of the 1970s.[2]

The demands of socialist realism for a positive and ideal representation of life would not easily fit the tragedy genre, although the climate was changing. Besides, finding a visual expression for the seriousness of the topic was not a simple task, neither was the search for a solution that would be smoothly adaptable to the studio production system. Zuikov's sketches were beautiful but not quickly reproducible, and Khitruk, trained as animator and mindful of the budget at hand, had no choice except to insist on simplifying his drawings, so that it would be easier to maintain their essence once the movement was added.[3]

DOI: 10.1201/9781003199625-7

BACKGROUND AND CHARACTERS

While searching for original stylistic solutions that would convey the mood of the film, Zuikov came up with a peculiar technique for the background: he saturated craft paper with sunflower oil until it became translucent; then, after placing a few layers on top of each other to create a feeling of depth, he would draw on them with charcoal. The characters were lighted from the top, while the background was illuminated from underneath, thus creating a yellowish quality that would convey depth and inner light. As Khitruk remembers, the stink of sunflower oil in the room was unbearable, but the result was incredible![4] The peculiar hue so obtained, which ranged from sepia to brown with crimson accents, perfectly complements the story and its solemn mood.

A sense of gravity also transpires through the subtle gestures and body language of the characters and affects the rhythm, which, even if it drags at times, succeeds in expressing the sobriety of the two protagonists' demeanors. By introducing the powerful animals in static scenes, the director offers a picture of their monolithic quality from the very inception. The bull stands in the middle of the prairie, unmoving, and releases a roar that reaches the lion, who looks impassible, a mirror image of the bull, strong, powerful, and majestic in his immobility.

In Khitruk's original idea the lion appears as a powerful mafia boss with a minion (the jackal) at his service.[5] The cliché was meant to convey a message in a condensed amount of time (as clichés always rely on an already established connection between the director's idea and the spectator's understanding), and function as a sort of parody.[6] The hint, though, is subtle, and the tragic quality of the film has the upper hand.

The somber atmosphere is jarred by the representation of the third character, the jackal. While the lion and the bull are depicted in a naturalistic way with realistic movements, the jackal is closer to Khitruk's idea of a "small little nasty dog with ears sticking up"[7] (Figures 6.1 and 6.2).

The character turned into a caricature, which would be humorous, if only the theme were not so tragic. His cartoonish style poorly suits the heavy atmosphere carefully woven throughout the film and clashes with the textured and soft background.

FIGURE 6.1 *The Lion and the Bull*. Lion and Bull. © Soyuzmultfilm.

Khitruk imagined the jackal as the character,

> which would wait every minute to be hit from behind or be ready to attack. He didn't have the same expression on his face not even for a moment: his face could be teary or show his teeth, scared or insolent.[8]

The director was deeply dissatisfied with the result and, in his usual modesty, only blamed himself, "I could imagine so clearly this transformation from scare to aggression, but none of this came out in the film. And this is my fault, because Sasha Dogorov is a very good animator and good actor."[9] Perhaps it was the friction caused by the characters being elaborated in different styles, or the lack of time to work on the film in more detail,[10] or the challenge to convey the complexity of the story on the screen without the use of dialogue that prevented the multifaceted intrigue in the story from transferring thoroughly into the film.[11] Still the drama seeps through the gravity of the lion and the bull, as well as through the setting, the music and the organization of the frame.

FIGURE 6.2 *The Lion and the Bull*. Jackal. Sketches. © Soyuzmultfilm.

A PROLOGUE IN CONDENSED FORM

From the very beginning, the film strings together images of a sorrowful landscape accompanied by a disquieting music. An uneasy mood is introduced in a subtle way, so that, as Khitruk believed, the viewer can subconsciously attune to the atmosphere demanded by the film and adopt the necessary psychological attitude.[12] A careful editing of long shots of the bull pulling a heavy weight, followed by close-ups of his head, eyes, and legs, prepares for the dramatic moment, when the bull, exhausted, finally collapses.[13] His fall does not detract from his dignified image. Once disengaged from the yoke and left behind in a pool of water, the bull gathers his strength to reach a hill. Here on its top, massive and solemn, his exhaustion and maybe inner turmoil is revealed by a simple detail: a single muscle twitches on his shoulder.[14] The whole scene functions, according to Khitruk, as a prologue in a condensed form.[15]

MORAL WITHOUT WORDS

From the beginning and throughout the film, Khitruk aimed to present his ideas in essential images devoid of any verbal code. Despite the absence of words, the moral of the film about the tragic outcomes in the quest for power still filters through, but Khitruk felt that the subtleties of the drama present in the original story were lost in the adaptation of the text.[16] Khitruk rarely uses dialogue in his films; instead, he often relies on a narrative voice. In this film, he completely removed any verbal communication. The absent dialogue is substituted only by the soundtrack. "It didn't fit," Khitruk recalls,

> Maybe it was a mistake. I wanted to get around the text. But without the text, it was difficult to convey the drama. [...] There is a very subtle game. It's Iago! Very subtle transitions. And I tried to squeeze in this drama, to concentrate it in a bouillon cube. It did not work out.[17]

At the end, after all characters succumb, only a colossal tree in the prairie is left behind. His shape resembles the nuclear mushroom, the ultimate symbol of destruction. Universal questions about human nature and the search for power materialize in a topical theme, yet Khitruk's intention goes beyond a contemporary political commentary. The film was not meant to be a political feuilleton, or provide a commentary on the cold war, or at least not only, but rather it was conceived as a parable exploring the complexity of the human mind and the delicate equilibrium of power.[18]

The tragic end of this film sounds like a warning for the spectators but at the same time points towards a still achievable ideal. As Khitruk would say, "if we talk about fear, it is to emphasize the precious moment in which one overcomes fear, overcomes oneself. Only then will the film do its job."[19] The film was not addressed exclusively to adults, but children as well. "We protect children from tragedies, not wanting to injure their psyche," says Khitruk,

That's right, baby souls are easily hurt. But much more often we traumatize them with reproaches, punishment, or the threat of punishment for offenses that they are not even aware of. The strength of a moral lesson, the entire system of moral values should be built in a way that the child himself determines the measure of his responsibility. In this respect, a story has great advantages over other forms of reprimands: it does not directly blame, it does not point the finger to anyone. Here is a story about a vile jackal – it's not about me, here I don't need to wriggle out or make excuses. Here I act as a judge and, unknowingly, judge myself.[20]

With *The Lion and the Bull* Khitruk tackled those universal questions that haunted him since his childhood and that, in one way or another, pervaded all his films, but here they are expressed without filters or censorship (inner or political). Despite Khitruk's dissatisfaction with the result, this film is a masterpiece and successfully expresses the culmination of Khitruk's decades-long search for the right form to express his ideas; and it is with this film that his extensive studies on movement reached an extreme.

In the final fighting scene, strokes freeze suspended on the screen, as though devoid of a corporeal entity; the animal bodies turn into lines of energy, shapes that intersect and transform until their mutual annihilation (Figure 6.3).

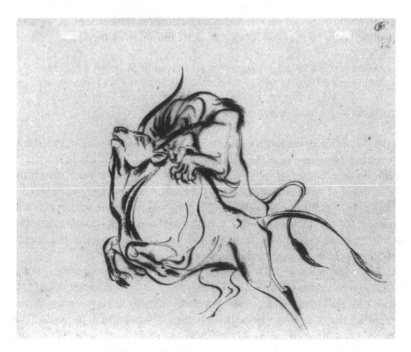

FIGURE 6.3 *The Lion and the Bull.* Fight scene. Sketch. © Soyuzmultfilm.

With this succession of static frames, Khitruk's search came to its apex, movements are distilled to their very essence. Now it was time to pass his knowledge and his mastery on to younger generations.

NOTES

1   Khitruk, "Vospominaniia," 11; Khitruk, *Professiia-animator*, 2007, 1: 18.
2   Best examples of this trend are the early *The Tale of Tale* (Iurii Norstein, 1979) or in stop-motion *Separated* (*Razluchennye*, Nikolai Serebriakov, 1980), but a general tendency developed later, towards the second half of the 1980s, in a search of roots and myths – *The Lodgers of an Old House* (*Zhil'tsy starogo doma*, Aleksei Karaev, 1988), *Whom to Tell My Sorrow?* (*Komu povem pechal' moiu?* Natal'ia Orlova, 1988), *Kutkh and the Mice* (*Kutkh i myshi*, Oksana Cherkasova, 1985, Sverdlovskaia kinostudiia), *How to Become a Man* (*Kak stat' chelovekom*, Vladimir Petkevich, 1988, Sverdlovskaia kinostudiia), *The Dream* (*Son*, Nina Shorina, 1988) – or a return to an archaic level of consciousness, expressed in both a representation of an ethnographic world or the rehabilitation of myths – *Night* (*Noch'*, Petkevich, 1984, Sverdlovskaia kinostudiia), *The Cow* (*Korova,* Aleksandr Petrov, 1989, Sverdlovskaia kinostudiia), *5/4* (Ivan Maksimov, 1990, Pilot), *Landscape with Juniper* (*Peizazh s mozhzhevelnikom*, Andrei Khrzhanovskii, 1987), *Kele* (Mikhail Aldashin, 1988). See discussion of these trends in Krivulia, *Labirinty animatsii.* Among Soviet republic studios, one of the most poignant films, *There Will Be Soft Rains* (*Budet Laskovyi Dozhd'*, Nazim Tuliakhodzhaev, 1984, O'zbekfilm/ Uzbekfil'm) combined tragedy and lyricism with a science-fiction twist.
3   Zuikov, "Vse reshila sluchainost'," 289.
4   Khitruk, *Professiia-animator*, 2007, 1: 289.
5   Khitruk, 1: 282.
6   Khitruk, 1: 282.
7   Zuikov, "Vse reshila sluchainost'," 290.
8   Khitruk, *Professiia-animator*, 2007, 1: 300.
9   Khitruk, 1: 300.
10 Khitruk, "Energiia poiska," 300.
11 Maliukova, "Poteriav, ne chuvstvoval sebia poteriannym."
12 Khitruk often uses the time dedicated to the credits to bring the spectator into the appropiate mood, since short films do not allow much time to create the introductory atmosphere. Khitruk, *Professiia-animator*, 2007, 1: 274.
13 Khitruk, 1: 274–75.
14 Khitruk, 1: 278.
15 Khitruk, 1: 275–76.
16 Khitruk, 1: 301.
17 Khitruk, 1: 302.
18 Khitruk, 1: 286.
19 Khitruk and Khaniutin, "Samoe 'detskoe' iskusstvo," 48.
20 Khitruk, *Professiia-animator*, 2007, 1: 18; Khitruk, "Vospominaniia," 11.

Conclusion
Khitruk – The Teacher

After *The Lion and the Bull*, Khitruk reached a turning point. He felt he had expressed in his films all he had desired to convey and was now ready to abandon the directorial role.[1] He began to collaborate as artistic director at the studio Mul'ttelefil'm (Èkran), and above all to devote himself wholeheartedly to teaching. The role of a pedagogue was not new to him; he had been teaching since 1956, when the studio assigned him a group of students to train in the profession.[2] But it was only at the beginning of the 1980s that specialized courses, "Secondary Courses for Screenwriters and Directors," were established at the studio Soyuzmultfilm, and Khitruk was one of the founders and teachers among other legendary personalities such as Norstein, Khrzhanovskii, Nazarov, Bardin, Kachanov, and Pekar'. Some of the most important and influential directors of the 1990s (such as Oksana Cherkasova, Mikhail Aldashin, Mikhail Tumelia, Aleksandr Petrov, and Ivan Maksimov, to name a few) emerged from these courses.

The end of the 1980s was characterized by an exceptional creative energy.[3] It was the time of the Perestroika, when the system could be stretched to accept new ideas. With the following collapse of the Soviet Union, the animation world started to change even more drastically. The ideological censorship was replaced by economic censorship and the process of adaptation to a new market-base world was a challenge for any form of art, if not the entire society. But despite the difficult times, in 1993, Khitruk, together with Andrei Khrzhanovskii, Iurii Norstein, and Eduard Nazarov, managed not only to found the school-studio SHAR (Shkola animatsionnoi rezhissury, School of Animation Direction), but also to release works of its students (some of the best films of the 1990s) and maintain a high-quality production.

Indeed, Khitruk was exceptionally dedicated to his students, not only because he desired to share his knowledge, but also because he realized, as the best teachers do, that it is by teaching that one can dig deeper and truly understand a subject.[4] He was eager to learn from his students as much as teach them. The students' creative individualities, experiences, perspectives, and styles inspired him;[5] their inquiries, he would say, were a way to evolve, to pose himself questions that he never thought about beforehand.[6] In testimonies and articles published by his students, Khitruk appears as the ideal teacher. He was a master in his profession, and he could convey his experience in an organized, simple, and accessible way. In addition, he was a good listener and mentor, relentlessly willing to guide his students to understand their inner motivations, to explore beyond the surface, and discover their own style.[7]

The courses Khitruk taught were based on "classical animation," which he defined as a kind of animation "founded on deep psychological development of the character and on the detailed and realistic development of the action."[8] Khitruk realized that classical animation was at that time considered by many as an old style, but he believed that it was a school of movement and acting that was at the base of the profession, and necessary to hone in order to maintain outstanding standards.[9] Despite the fact that Khitruk's formation derived from the established Disney style, he evolved as a director following "anti-Disney" tendencies. Even in his teaching he emphasized the need to value the fundamental lessons of traditional cel animation and then move forward from there.[10]

With a desire to pass along his knowledge, Khitruk spent decades writing a book about the profession of animator (*Professiia-animator*, 2007), which is a precious heritage for any animator. In this study, Khitruk drew from different realms – visual art, theater, literature, poetry, and literary theory – in an attempt to unravel an underlying system that could express those visual solutions that often came to him by an innate intuition but that his analytical mind repeatedly urged him to systematize. He strived to find a language that would explain his work as animator, but which, at times, proves to be futile in addressing that intangible quality in art that eschews rationalization. The process caused him much frustration; however, it also made him an exceptional teacher and mentor.

Khitruk constantly looked back at his own experience as well as at the practice of his foreign colleagues, to the extent that in the 1990s he compiled an international dictionary of animation terms and translated into Russian Whitaker and Halas's book *Timing in Animation*,[11] and Leonard Maltin's book *Of Mice and Magic*,[12] which was published posthumously in 2018.

Khitruk fulfilled the roles not only of animator, director, translator, scriptwriter,[13] and pedagogue, but also of protector of younger artists. As the writer Liudmila Petrushevskaya explains, Khitruk was like an ambassador, or "an infiltrator within the system, working for the other side, that is for us."[14] It is thanks to him that innovative films could be realized. He was admired by the young generation and respected by the authorities. He fulfilled the role of mediator, softening the state directives and smoothing the way for young people.[15] He was a master, an innovator, a teacher, and a pillar for many animators. With them his legacy continues.

NOTES

1   The tragic loss of his wife in 1984 might also have contributed to the decision to take a pause or a leave from the directorial role. Maliukova, "Poteriav, ne chuvstvoval sebia poteriannym." Only on August 11, 1988, did Khitruk remarry with Galina Nikolaevna Shvedova (Khitruk).

2   Khitruk, *Professiia-animator*, 2007, 2: 9.

3   Khitruk, 2: 19.

4   Khitruk, *Professiia-animator*, 2007, 2: 9.

5   Khitruk, 2: 26.

6   Khitruk, 2: 9.

7   Aldashin, "O Khitruke," 276–77. Petrov and Tumelia, "Nauka udivliat'," 266.

8   Khitruk, *Professiia-animator*, 2007, 2: 29–30.

9   Khitruk, 2: 30.

10   Khitruk, 2: 102.

11   Whitaker and Halas, *Timing for Animation*. Khitruk's translation: Uayteker and Khalas, *Taiming v animatsii*.

12   Maltin, *Of Mice and Magic*. Translated by Khitruk: Maltin, *O myshakh i magii. Istoriia amerikanskogo risovannogo fil'ma.*

13   Apart from working on the scripts for his films, Khitruk wrote the script for *The Tale of the Prince and the Three Doctors* (Oksana Tkachenko, 1965, Kyivnaukfilm/Kievnauchfil'm), *Three Stories* (Elena Barinova, 1986), and a script never realized, which only recently was published in the journal Iskusstvo Kino, see Khitruk, "Prodaetsia zemlia. Stsenarii animatsionnogo fil'ma."

14   *The Spirit of Genius.*

15   See Kleiman's comments on Khitruk in *The Spirit of Genius.*

Films Cited

All films were released by Soyuzmultfilm unless indicated.

25th the First Day (25-oe - pervyi den'). Directed by Iurii Norstein, Arkadii Tiurin. 1968.

5/4. Directed by Ivan Maksimov. 1990. Pilot.

And I Am Again with You (I s vami snova ia). Directed by Andrei Khrzhanovskii. 1980.

Animated Crocodile N. 1 (Muk. Mul'tiplikatsionnyi krokodil. N.1). Directed by Vladimir Pekar', Vladimir Popov, Lev Pozdneev. 1960.

Arkhangelsk Stories (Arkhangel'skie novelly). Directed by Leonid Nosyrev. 1986.

At the Back Desk (Na zadnei parte). Directed by Valerii Ugarov. 1978.

Autumn (Osen'). Directed by Andrei Khrzhanovskii. 1982.

Ave Maria. Directed by Ivan Ivanov-Vano, Vladimir Danilevich. 1972.

A Badly Painted Hen (Špatně namalovaná slepice). Directed by Jiří Brdečka. 1963. Krátký Film, Bratři v triku.

Balance of Fear (Ravnovesie strakha). Directed by Eduard Nazarov, Vladimir Zuikov, Fëdor Khitruk. 1973.

The Ballad of the Table (Ballada o stole). Directed by Mikhail Kalinin, Roman Davydov. 1955.

Ballet mécanique. Directed by Fernand Léger. 1924. Synchro-Ciné.

Bambi. Directed by James Algar, Samuel Armstrong, David Hand. 1942. Walt Disney Productions.

The Band Concert. Directed by Wilfred Jackson. 1935. Walt Disney Productions.

The Bathhouse (Bania). Directed by Anatolii Karanovich, Sergei Yutkevich. 1962.

The Battle of Kerzhenets (Secha pri Kerzhentse). Directed by Iurii Norstein, Ivan Ivanov-Vano. 1971.

The Battleship Potëmkin (Bronenosets Potemkin). Directed by Sergei Eisenstein. 1925. Mosfil'm. Goskino.

Bazaar, Scene from the Tale of the Pope and His Worker Balda (Bazar - Skazka o pope i rabotnike ego Balda). Directed by Mikhail Tsekhanovskii. 1936.

The Blue Puppy (Goluboi shchenok). Directed by Efim Gamburg. 1976.

A Brave Sailor (Otvazhnyi moriak). Directed by Viktor Smirnov. 1936. Soiuzdetmul'tfil'm.

Bremen musicians (Bremenskie muzykanty). Directed by Inessa Kovalevskaia. 1969.

A Cat and a Half (Poltora kota). Directed by Andrei Khrzhanovskii. 2002. Dago Kompaniia.

Cheburasha Goes to School (Cheburashka idet v shkolu). Directed by Roman Kachanov. 1983.

Cheburashka. Directed by Roman Kachanov. 1971.

The Circus. Directed by Charles Chaplin. 1928. Charles Chaplin Productions.

The Circus (Tsirk). Directed by Grigorii Alexandrov. 1936. Mosfil'm.

143

Cossacks (Kozaki). Series. Directed by Volodymyr Dakhno. 1967. Kyivnaukfilm/ Kievnauchfil'm.

The Cranes are Flying (Letiat zhuravli). Directed by Mikhail Kalatozov. 1957. Mosfil'm.

The Cow (Korova). Directed by Aleksandr Petrov. 1989. Sverdlovskaia Kinostudiia.

Curiosity (Znatiželja). Directed by Borivoj (Bordo) Dovniković. 1966. Zagreb Film.

The Dream (Son). Directed by Nina Shorina. 1988.

A Drop Too Much (O skleničku víc). Directed by Břetislav Pojar. 1954. Krátký Film Praha, Loutkový Film Praha.

Dumbo. Directed by Samuel Armstrong, Norman Ferguson, Wilfred Jackson. 1941. Walt Disney Productions.

Dzhiabzha. Directed by Mstislav Pashchenko. 1938. Lenfil'm.

Emergency Aid (Skoraia pomoshch'). Directed by Lamis Bredis. 1948.

Eralash. Directed by Aleksandr Khmelik, Boris Grachevskii, Alla Surikova, Aleksei Rybnikov. 1974–1996. Gor'ky Fil'm.

Fedia Zaitsev. Directed by Valentina and Zinaida Brumberg. 1948.

Fitil'. An All-Union Satirical Cinematic Journal. 1962–1990. Mosfil'm, Studiia im. Gor'kogo,

Four from a Backyard (Chetvero s odnogo dvora). Directed by Inessa Kovalevskaia. 1967.

Frantishek. Directed by Vadim Kurchevskii. 1967.

Gena the Crocodile (Krokodil Gena). Directed by Roman Kachanov. 1969.

The Glass Harmonica (Stekliannaia garmonika). Directed by Andrei Khrzhanovskii. 1968.

The Great Relay (Bol'shaia estafeta). Directed by Ivan Aksenchuk. 1979.

The Hand (Ruka). Directed by Jiří Trnka. 1965. Krátký Film Praha, Loutkový Film Praha.

Hell (Põrgu). Directed by Rein Raamat. 1983. Tallinnfilm.

How the Cossacks Became Olympians (Iak kozaki olimpiitsiami stali/Kak Kazaki olimpiitsami stali). Directed by Volodymyr Dakhno. 1978. Kyivnaukfilm/ Kievnauchfil'm.

How to Become a Man (Kak stat' chelovekom). Directed by Vladimir Petkevich. 1988. Sverdlovskaia Kinostudiia.

I Fly to You Like a Memory (Ia k vam lechu vospominaniem). Directed by Andrei Khrzhanovskii. 1977.

If You Don't Like It, Do Not Listen (Ne liubo - ne slushai). Directed by Leonid Nosyrev. 1977.

It Is in Our Power (Eto v nashikh silakh). Directed by Lev Atamanov. 1970.

Jealousy (Revnost). Directed by Todor Dinov. 1963. Boyana Film.

Just You Wait! (Nu Pogodi!). Directed by Viacheslav Kotenochkin. 1969–1993.

Karlson Returned (Karlson vernulsia). Directed by Boris Stepantsev. 1970.

Kele. Directed by Mikhail Aldashin, Peep Pedmanson. 1988.

The Kid and Karlson (Malysh i Karlson). Directed by Boris Stepantsev. 1968.

Kutkh and the Mice (Kutkh i myshi). Directed by Oksana Cherkasova. 1985. Sverdlovskaia Kinostudiia.

The Idea (L'idée). Directed by Berthold Bartosch. 1932. France. Maria Bartosch & Cecile Starr.

The Left-Handed Craftsman (Levsha). Directed by Ivan Ivanov-Vano, Vladimir Danilevich. 1964.

The Little Humpbacked Horse (Konek-Gorbunok). Directed by Ivan Ivanov-Vano, Aleksandra Snezhko-Blotskaia, Viktor Gromov. 1947.

The Little Humpbacked Horse. Remake (Konek-Gorbunok). Directed by Ivan Ivanov-Vano. 1975.

The Lodgers of an Old House (Zhil'tsy starogo doma). Directed by Aleksei Karaev. 1988.

The Long Journey (Dolgoe puteshestvie). Directed by Andrei Khrzhanovskii. 1997. Shkola-Studiia Shar.

The Magical Ring (Volshebnoe kol'tso). Directed by Leonid Nosyrev. 1979.

The Many Adventures of Winnie the Pooh. Directed by John Lounsbery, Wolfgang Reitherman. 1977. Walt Disney Productions.

Maugli (series). Directed by Roman Davydov. 1967–1971.

The Merry Circus (Veselý Cirkus). Directed by Jiří Trnka. 1951. Krátký Film Praha.

The Merry Go Round (Veselaia karusel'). 1969–2002.

Meteor in the Ring (Meteor na ringe). Directed by Boris Dëzhkin. 1970.

Moonbird. Directed by John Hubley, Elliott Faith. 1959. Faith and John Hubley -Storyboard Production.

My Favorite Time (Liubimoe moe vremia). Directed by Andrei Khrzhanovskii. 1987.

Neighbours. Directed by Norman McLaren, 1952. National Film Board of Canada.

Night (Noch'). Directed by Vladimir Petkevich. 1984. Sverdlovskaia Kinostudiia.

The Nutcracker (Shchelkunchik). Directed by Boris Stepantsev. 1973.

Oh Sport, You Are Peace! (O sport - ty mir!). Directed by Iurii Ozerov. 1980. Mosfil'm.

Olympics-80 (Series - Olimpiade-80). Directed by Oleg Churkin, Rasa Strautmane, Boris Akulinichev, Anatolii Reznikov. 1980. Ekran.

On the Trail of the Bremen Town Musicians (Po sledam Bremenskikh muzykantov). Directed by Vasilii Livanov. 1973.

Operation x-70. Directed by Raoul Servais. 1971. Pen Films.

The Origin of the Species (Proiskhozhdenie vida). Directed by Efim Gamburg. 1966.

Peace to Your House (Mir domu tvoemu). Directed by Viktor Nikitin, Igor' Nikolaev. 1962.

Peculiar Penguins. Directed by Wilfred Jackson. 1934. Walt Disney Productions.

Pencil and Blot - Happy Hunters (Karandash i kliaksa - veselie okhotniki). Directed by Evgenii Migunov. 1954.

Pinocchio. Directed by Norman Ferguson, Wilfred Jackson, T. Hee. 1940. Walt Disney.

The Political Satirical Journal (Zhurnal politsatiry). Directed by Dmitrii Babichenko, Ivan Ivanov-Vano, Aleksandr Ivanov, Vladimir Polkovnikov, Leonid Amal'rik. 1941.

Popeye the Sailor Meets Ali Baba's Forty Thieves. Directed by Dave Fleischer, Willard Bowsky, Jack Mercer, Mae Questel, Lou Fleischer. 1937. Fleischer Studios.

The Post (Pochta). Directed by Mikhail Tsekhanovskii. 1929. Leningradskaia Fabrika Sovkino.

The Post (Pochta) Remake. Directed by Mikhail Tsekhanovskii. 1964.

Puck! Puck! (Shaibu! Shaibu!). Directed by Boris Dëzhkin. 1964.

Rain (Dozhd'). Directed by Leonid Nosyrev. 1978.

Rematch (Match-revansh). Directed by Boris Dëzhkin. 1968.

Room and a Half, or Sentimental Journey to the Motherland (Poltory komnaty, ili sentimental'noe puteshestvie na rodinu). Directed by Andrei Khrzhanovskii. 2008. Kino-Studiia SHAR.

School of Fine Arts (Shkola iziashchnykh iskusstv). Directed by Andreii Khrzhanovskii. 1990.

School of Fine Arts. Landscape with Juniper (Shkola iziashchnykh iskusstv. Peizazh s mozhzhevel'nikom). Directed by Andrei Khrzhanovskii, Valerii Ugarov. 1987.

School of Fine Arts. Return (Shkola iziashchnykh iskusstv. Vozvrashchenie). Directed by Andrei Khrzhanovskii. 1990.

Seasons (Vremena goda). Directed by Ivan Ivanov-Vano, Iurii Norstein. 1969.

Separated (Razluchennye). Directed by Nikolai Serebriakov. 1980.

Shapokliak. Directed by Roman Kachanov. 1974.

The Shepherd Girl and the Chimney-Sweep (Pastushka i trubochist). Directed by Lev Atamanov. 1965.

The Signature is Illegible (Podpis' nerazborchiva). Directed by Aleksandr Ivanov, Lev Pozdneev. 1954.

The Snails (Les escargots). Directed by René Laloux. 1966. Sofac. The Criterion Collection.

Snow White and the Seven Dwarfs. Directed by William Cottrell, David Hand, Wilfred Jackson. 1938. Walt Disney Productions.

Song of the Prairie (Árie prérie). Directed by Jiří Trnka. 1949. Ceskoslovenský Státní Film, Loutkovy Film Praha.

Songs of Fiery Years (Pesni ognennykh let). Directed by Inessa Kovalenskaia. 1971.

Soon There Will Be Rain (Skoro budet dozhd'). Directed by Vladimir Polkovnikov. 1959.

Strange Bird (Strannaia ptitsa). Directed by Borivoj Dovniković. 1969. Zagreb Film.

Tale of Tales (Skazka skazok). Directed by Iurii Norstein. 1979.

The Tale of Igor's Campaign (Skazannia pro Igoriv pokhid/Skazanie pro Igorev poxod). Directed by Nina Vasilenko. 1972. Kyivnaukfilm/Kievnauchfil'm.

The Tale of the Prince and the Three Doctors (Skazka o tsareviche i trekh lekariakh). Directed by Oksana Tkachenko, written by Fëdor Khitruk. 1965. Kyivnaukfilm/Kievnauchfil'm.

The Tale of the Old Oak (Skazka starogo duba). Directed by Ol'ga Khodataeva. 1949.

There Will Be Soft Rains (Budet laskovyi dozhd'). Directed by Nazim Tuliakhodzhaev. 1984. O'zbekfilm/Uzbekfil'm.

Three Little Pigs. Directed by Burt Gillet. 1933. Walt Disney Productions.

Three Stories (Tri novelly). Directed by Elena Barinova. 1986.

The Three from Prostokvashino (Troe iz prostokvashino). Directed by Vladimir Popov. 1978.

Uncle Stëpa - Policeman (Diadia Stëpa - militsioner). Directed by Ivan Aksenchuk. 1964.

Vacations in Prostokvashino (Kanikuly v Prostokvashino). Directed by Vladimir Popov. 1980.

Varezhka. Directed by Roman Kachanov. 1967.

The Villain with a Label (Zlodeika s nakleikoi). Directed by Boris Stepantsev, Vsevolod Shcherbakov. 1954.

The Wall (Zid). Directed by Ante Zaninović. 1966. Zagreb Film.

The Wheel of Fortune (Koleso fortuny). Directed by Anatolii Solin. 1980. Ekran.

Who said Miaow (Kto skazal miau?). Directed by Vladimir Degtiarev. 1962.

Whom to Tell My Sorrow? (Komu povem pechal' moiu?). Directed by Natal'ia Orlova. 1988.

Winnie the Pooh and the Blustery Day. Directed by Wolfgang Reitherman. 1968. Walt Disney Productions.

Winnie the Pooh and the Honey Tree. Directed by Wolfgang Reitherman. 1966. Walt Disney Productions.

Winnie the Pooh and Tigger Too. Directed by John Lounsbery, Wolfgang Reitherman. 1974. Walt Disney Productions.

Winter in Prostokvashino (Zima v Prostokvashino). Directed by Vladimir Popov. 1984.

Yellow Submarine. Directed by George Dunning. 1968. TVC London. King Features.

Zigzag of Success (Zigzag udachi). Directed by El'dar Riazanov. 1968. Mosfil'm.

DOCUMENTARY FILMS AND PODCASTS ABOUT KHITRUK

Animation from A to Z. Series 7–10, 18 (Animatsiia ot A do IA. Seriia 7–10, 18). Directed by Irina Margolina, M. Liakhovetsky. 1997.

Fëdor Khitruk. Portrait of an Artist and His Era. Film 9 (Fëdor Khitruk. Portret khudozhnika na fone epokhi). Directed by Irina Margolina. 2014. Studio M.I.R.

Fëdor Khitruk. Profession - Animator (Fëdor Khitruk. Professiia-animator). Directed by Sergei Serëgin. 1999. Shkola-Studiia Animatsionnogo Kino SHAR - Master-Fil'm.

Fëdor Khitruk. To Be Everything. (Fëdor Khitruk. Byt' vsem). Directed by Dmitrii Zolotov. 2017. Studia Master-Fil'm.

Magia Russica. Directed by Yonathan Zur, Masha Zur. 2004. Yonathan & Masha Films.

Miracle Factory. Part 3 Art Director (Fabrika chudes. Khudozhnik postanovshchik. 3). Directed by Aleksei Vakrushev. 2006. Tsentr natsional'nogo fil'ma.

Portraits of the Era. Fëdor Khitruk (Portrety epokhi. Fëdor Khitruk). Directed by Anna Iarovenko. 2002. Vertov i Ko, Telekanal Rossiia, RGTRK. https://www.culture.ru/live/movies/2913/portrety-epokhi-fyodor-khitruk.

S Khitrukom ushla tselaia vselennaia. 2012. Novosti. Novosti. NTV. https://www.ntv.ru/novosti/378416/

Soyuzmultfilm - Tales and True Stories. First Episode. Old Walls (series - Soyumul'tfil'm - Skazki i byli. Starye steny). Directed by Natalia Lukinykh. 2003. Fond sotsial'no-kul'turnykh program Guberniia.

Soyuzmultfilm - Tales and True Stories. Second Episode. Khitruk and All, All, All (series - Soyumul'tfil'm - Skazki i byli. Khitruk i vse vse vse). Directed by Natalia Lukinykh. 2003. 26 min. Fond sotsial'no-kul'turnykh program Guberniia.

The Spirit of Genius. Directed by Otto Alder. 1998. Tag/Traum.

Weightless Life (Nevesomaia zhizn'). Directed by Liubov' Khobotova. 2006. Studiia SVS, GTRK Kul'tura.

Films Directed by Fëdor Khitruk and Awards

STORY OF A CRIME (ISTORIIA ODNOGO PRESTUPLENIIA, 1962)

"Golden Gate" Award for Best Animated Film for Adults, San Francisco International
  Film Festival, USA, 1963
First Prize in the animation category, All-Union Film Festival, Leningrad, USSR, 1964
Prize of the International Jury, Oberhausen International Short Film Festival, FRG,
  1963

TOPTYZHKA (1964)

San Marco Lion for Best Film for Children, Venice Film Festival, Italy, 1964

BONIFATIUS'S VACATION (KANIKULY BONIFATSIIA, 1965)

First Prize in the Category of Animation, All-Union Film Festival, Kiev, Ukrainian
  SSR, 1966
"Golden Pelican" Prize for Animated Films for Children, International Animation
  Film Festival, Mamaia, Romania, 1966
Honorary Diploma, Cork International Film Festival, Ireland, 1965
Award, International Festival of Films for Children, Teheran, Iran, 1967

WINNIE THE POOH SERIES (*VINNI PUKH*, 1969–72)

USSR State award to Fëdor Khitruk for all films of the series *Winnie the Pooh and All... (Vinni Pukh i vse vse vse...)*, USSR, 1976

OTHELLO 67 (*OTHELLO-67*, 1967)

ASIFA Special Award, Annecy International Animation Film Festival, France, 1967

FILM FILM FILM (*FIL'M, FIL'M, FIL'M*, 1968)

Silver Medal, Animation Festival New York, USA, 1973
Diploma of Merit, Tampere Film Festival, Finland, 1970
Award, Oberhausen International Short Film Festival, FGR, 1969
Award for Best Short Film, Colombo International Film Festival, Sri Lanka, 1973

THE YOUNG FRIEDRICH ENGELS (*IUNOSHA FRIDRIK ENGELS*, FËDOR KHITRUK, VADIM KURCHEVSKII, KATIA GEORGI, CLAUS GEORGI, 1970)

"Golden Dove," International Film Festival, Leipzig, GDR, 1970
Prize of the International Jury, Oberhausen International Short Film Festival, FGR, 1971
Art Prize of the German Democratic Republic (DDR Kunstpreis) to Fëdor Khitruk and Vadim Kurchevskii, GDR, 1971

BALANCE OF FEAR (RAVNOVESIE STRAHA, EDUARD NAZAROV, VLADIMIR ZUIKOV, FËDOR KHITRUK, 1973)

Prize, Oberhausen International Short Film Festival, FGR, 1976

THE ISLAND (OSTROV, 1973)

"Palme d'Or for Short Film," Cannes Film Festival, France, 1974
Animation Second Prize, All-Union Film Festival, Baku, Azerbaijan SSR, 1974
"The Golden Dragon," and CIDALC Honorary Diploma, Krakow Film Festival, Poland, 1974

I'LL GIVE YOU A STAR (DARIU TEBE ZVEZDU, 1974)

Special Jury Prize for Short Film, Cannes Film Festival, France, 1975
Collective Award, All-Union Film Festival, Kishinev, Moldavian SSR, 1975

ICARUS AND THE WISEMEN (IKAR I MUDRETSY, 1976)

Animation Second Prize, All-Union Film Festival, Riga, Latvian SSR, 1977
Children's Film Award, Annecy International Animation Film Festival, France, 1977

OLYMPICS (OLIMPIONIKI, 1982)

USSR State Prize for the animation in the film *Oh Sport, You are Peace!* (*O sport – ty mir!* Iurii Ozerov, 1980), USSR, 1982

THE LION AND THE BULL (LEV I BYK, 1983)

Audience Award, Ottawa International Animation Festival in Toronto, Canada, 1984
Award for Best Animation, Tampere Film Festival, Finland, 1984
Special Mention from the International Jury, International Animated Film Festival of Espinho, Portugal, 1984

FËDOR KHITRUK HONORS AND AWARDS

1976 USSR State Prize to the director Fëdor Khitruk for the films *I'll Give You a Star, The Island, Film Film Film,* and *Winnie-the-Pooh* series
1987 People's Artist of the USSR
1987 Findling Award (Findlingspreis) for Khitruk's life work, GDR
1997 Laureate of the Prize V. Starevich, USSR
1998 Prize of the President of the Russian Federation in the Field of Literature and Art
2001 Prize of the President of the Russian Federation "For contribution to cinema"
2002 Prize of the National Academy of Cinematographic Arts and Sciences of Russia "Golden Eagle"
2005 Award "For contribution to the profession," Open Russian Festival of Animation, Suzdal', USSR
2006 Lifetime Achievement Award, World Festival of Animated Films, Zagreb, Croatia
2006 Nika Award - Special Prize of the Academy Council "For outstanding contribution to Russian Cinema," USSR

Vice-president ASIFA (1980–1988)
Honorary President of the Russian International Animated Film Festival "Golden Fish" (since 1996)
Honorary President of the Russian Animated Film Association (1996–2000).
Honorary Professor of the Russian State University of Cinematography (VGIK), (2002).
Member of the Russian Academy of Cinematography "Nika".

Selected Bibliography

Aldashin, Mikhail. "O Khitruke." In *Professiia-animator*, edited by Fëdor Khitruk, 275–277. Moscow: Live Book, 2008.

Aldoshina, O. "Pushkinskaia trilogiia Andreia Khrzhanovskogo." *Iskusstvo kino* 7 (1997): 72–75.

Alimov, Sergei. "Rezervy mul'tiplikatsii." *Tvorchestvo* 9 (1967): 18.

Alimov, Sergei, and Vladimir Serebrovskii. *Sergei Alimov: Teatr Kino Grafika. Katalog Vystavki*. Moscow: Sovetskii khudozhnik, 1983.

Andersen, Hans Christian. *Fairy Tales*. New York: Scribner, 1950.

Anisimov, Grigorii. "Zaichik solnechnyi v zerkale pliashet. Grafika Sergeia Alimova." *Literaturnoe obozrenie* 3 (1980): 91–92.

Asenin, Sergei. "Sovremennye volshebniki ekrana." *Iskusstvo kino* 10 (1962): 62–68.

———. "Nakazanie smekhom." *Iskusstvo kino* 4 (1963): 100–104.

———. "Vozmozhnosti mul'tiplikatsii." *Iskusstvo kino* 8 (1964): 56–63.

———. "Vozmozhnosti mul'tiplikatsii." *Iskusstvo kino* 7 (1966): 40–43.

———. "Mudrost' vymysla." *Iskusstvo kino* 6 (1968): 44–57.

———. *Volshebniki ekrana. Esteticheskie problemy sovremennoi mul'tiplikatsiia*. Moscow: Iskusstvo, 1974.

———. "Smeshnoe i vysokoe." In *Ekran 79/80*, 78–81. Moscow: Iskusstvo, 1982.

———, ed. *Mudrost' vymysla. Mastera mul'tiplikatsii o sebe i svoem iskusstve*. Moscow: Iskusstvo, 1983.

———. *Mir mul'tfil'ma*. Moscow: Iskusstvo, 1986.

Atamanov, Lev. "Protiv naturalizma." *Iskusstvo kino* 5 (1959): 123–124.

Babichenko, Dmitrii. "Privet druz'iam." *Iskusstvo kino* 7 (1957): 9–16.

———. "Dovol'no mul'tshtampov." *Iskusstvo kino* 10 (1961a): 32–43.

———. "Talantlivo, ostroumno!" *Iskusstvo kino* 12 (1961b): 62–65.

———. *Iskusstvo mul'tiplikatsii*. Moscow: Iskusstvo, 1964.

———. *Mastera sovetskoi mul'tiplikatsii. Sbornik statei*. Moscow: Iskusstvo, 1972.

Bakhtin, Mikhail. "Forms of Time and of the Chronotope in the Novel. Notes toward a Historical Poetics." In *The Dialogic Imagination. Four Essays*, edited by Michael Holquist, 84–258. Austin: University of Texas Press, 1981.

Bardin, Garri. "'Mul'tiki - eto kirpichi zhizni.' Interview with Garri Bardin." Momenty, March 9, 2016. https://momenty.org/people/i162812/.

Belousov, Iu. *Fil'my - skazki. 11. Fil'my-skazki*. Moscow: Iskusstvo, 1979.

Bendazzi, Giannalberto. *Animation: A World History. Contemporary Times*. 3 vols. Boca Raton, FL: CRC Press, Taylor & Francis Group, 2016.

Bergson, Henri. *Laughter : An Essay on the Meaning of the Comic*. Translated by Cloudesley Brereton and Fred Rothwell. Copenhagen; Los Angeles, CA: Green Integer, 1999.

Beumers, Birgit. "Comforting Creatures in Children's Cartoons." In *Russian Children's Literature and Culture*, edited by Marina Balina and Larissa Rudova, 153–171. New York: Routledge, 2007.

Boiarsky, Iosif Iakovlevich. *Literaturnye kollazhi*. Tsentr psikhologii i psikhoterapii, 1996.

Borodin, Georgii. *"Animatsiia podnevol'naia."* Moscow, n.d.

———. "Skoraia pomoshch'. Iz istorii mu'tfil'ma Medvedkina." *Kinovedcheskie zapiski* 49 (2000): 83–85.

———. "Animatsiia podnevol'naia." *Kinograf* 16 (2005a): 54–153.

———. "V bor'be za malen'kie mysli. Neadekvatnost' tsenzury (glava iz knigi "Animatsiia podnevol'naia)." *Kinovedcheskie zapiski* 73 (2005b): 261–309.

———. "Olimpiada pod znakom medvedia." *Seance* 55/56 (February 7, 2014). https://seance.ru/articles/olympics_animation/.

———. "'Za Den' do nashei ery' - zaiavka i istoriia." *Seance*, May 1, 2020. https://seance.ru/articles/day-before-explication-archive/.

Boym, Svetlana. *Common Places: Mythologies of Everyday Life in Russia*. Cambridge, MA: Harvard University Press, 1994.

Bruegel the Elder, Pieter. *The Parable of the Blind*. 1568. Distemper on linen, 86x154 cm. Naples, Italy: Museo di Capodimonte.

Chegodaev, A. D. *Stranitsy istorii sovetskoi zhivopisi i sovetskoi grafiki*. Moskva: Izdatel'stvo sovetskii khudozhnik, 1984.

Chekhov, Anton. "Chelovek v futliare." In *Sobranie sochinenii v 8-mi tomakh*, 6: 259–271. Moscow: Pravda, 1969.

David, Jacques Louis. *The Royal Tennis Court Oath at Versailles on June 29, 1789*. n.d. Fresco (unfinished). 1791–1792. Musée national du Château de Versailles et de Trianon.

Doane, Mary Ann. *The Desire to Desire: The Woman's Film of the 1940s*. Series Theories of Representation and Difference. Bloomington: Indiana University Press, 1987.

Eisenstein, Sergei. *Izbrannye proizvedeniia*. Vol. 6. Moscow: Iskusstvo, 1964a.

———. "Viatskaia loshadka." In *Izbrannye proizvedeniia v shesti tomakh*, 3: 500–514. Moscow: Iskusstvo, 1964b.

———. "Za kadrom." In *Izbrannye proizvedeniia v shesti tomakh*, 2: 283–296. Moscow: Iskusstvo, 1964c.

———. "Disnei (publikatsiia i kommentarii N. I. Kleimana)." In *Problemy sinteza v khudozhestvennoi kul'ture*, edited by Anatolii Prokhorov, Boris Raushenbakh, and Fëdor Khitruk, 209–284. Moskva: Nauka, 1985.

———. "From Lectures on Music and Colour in *Ivan The Terrible*. 1947." In *The Eisenstein Reader*, edited by Richard Taylor, 167–186. London: BFI Publishing, 1998a.

———. "The Montage of Attractions." In *The Eisenstein Reader*, edited by Richard Taylor, 29–34. London: BFI Publishing, 1998b.

———. "The Montage of Film Attractions." In *The Eisenstein Reader*, edited by Richard Taylor, 35–52. London: BFI Publishing, 1998c.

———. "Zametki ob iskusstve Uolta Disneia." *Kinovedcheskie zapiski* 52 (2001): 98–114.

————. "Charlie the Kid." In *Metod. Tom vtoroi. Tainy masterov stat'i i etyudi*, edited by Naum Kleiman, 2: 226–253. Moscow: Muzei Kino. Eizenstein-tsentr, 2002a.

————. "Disnei." In *Metod. Tom vtoroi. Tainy masterov stat'i i etyudi*, edited by Naum Kleiman, 2: 255–295. Moscow: Muzey Kino. Eizenstein-tsentr, 2002b.

————. *Eisenstein on Disney*, edited by Jay Leyda, translated by Alan Upchurch. London: Seagull Books, 2017.

Elizarov, Georgii. *Sovetskaia mul'tiplikatsiia. Spravochnik*. Moscow: Komitet po kinematografii pri sovete ministrov SSSR Gosfil'mofond, 1966.

Elphick, Daniel. "Cartoon Time." *Lines That Have Escaped Destruction. Researching the Life and Music of Mieczysław Weinberg* (blog), April 25, 2013. http://linesthathaveescapeddestruction.blogspot.com/2013/04/cartoon-time.html.

————. "Vinni Pukh." *Lines That Have Escaped Destruction. Researching the Life and Music of Mieczysław Weinberg* (blog), October 26, 2016. http://linesthathaveescapeddestruction.blogspot.com/2016/10/vinni-pukh.html.

Epstein, Jean. "For a New Avant-Garde." In *French Film Theory and Criticism. A History, Anthology. 1907–1939*, edited by Richard Abel, 1: 349–353. Princeton, NJ: Princeton University Press, 1988.

Evteeva, Irina Vsevolodovna. "Protsess zhanroobrazovaniia v sovetskoi mul'tiplikatsii 60–80x godov. Avtoreferat." Leningradskii gosudarstvennyi institut teatra, muzyki i kinematografii imena N. K. Cherkasova (NIO), 1990.

Fedorova, L., and O. Shbina. *Katalog mul'tiplikatsionnykh kinofil'mov*. Moscow: Gos. Kom-t SSSR po televideniiu i radioveshchaniiu, Vses. Fond televizionnykh i radioprogramm, 1979.

"Fëdoru Khitruku-95." Vesti.ru, May 1, 2012. https://www.vesti.ru/article/1925349.

Foregger, Nikolai, Lev Kuleshov, and Aleksandr Rodchenko. "Charli Chaplin." *Kino-fot* 3 (1922): 2–6.

Ginzburg, Semen. "Sovetskaia mul'tiplikatsiia v borbe za realizm." In *Voprosy kinoiskusstva. Sbornik statei*, edited by Iu S. Kalashnikov, 381–411. Moscow: Gosudarstvennoe izdatel'stvo Iskusstvo, 1955.

————. "'Toptyzhka', ili vozvrashchennye emotsii detstva." *Iskusstvo kino* 4 (1965): 25–26.

Goder, Dina. "Moving Picture. The Little Known History of Russian Animation." *Russian Life* 46, no. 6 (2003): 24–31.

Golovanov, Vladimir. "Put' prostoty." In *Professiia-animator*, edited by Fëdor Khitruk, 2: 281–282. Moscow: Gaiatri, 2007.

Goskino. *Annotirovannyi katalog mul'tiplikatsionnykh i kukol'nykh fil'mov*. Moscow: Goskino RSFSR. Glavnoe upravlenie kinofikatsii i kinoprokata. Mosgorkinoprokat, 1982.

"Govoriat mastera mul'tiplikatsii." *Iskusstvo kino* 3 (1962): 130–142.

Gromov, Evgenii. *S. Alimov: mul'tiplikatsiia, knizhnaia i stankovaia grafika*. Mastera sovetskogo iskusstva. Moskva: Sovetskii khudozhnik, 1990.

Guliev, A. "Napriamik." *Iskusstvo kino* 8 (1962): 96–98.

Gurevich, Mikhail. "Pokadrovoe chtenie: literatura i animatsiia." *Kinovedcheskie zapiski* 6 (1990): 100–111.

Halas, John. *Art in Movement: New Directions in Animation*. New York: Hastings House, 1970.

Iampol'skii, Mikhail. "Prostranstvo mul'tiplikatsii." *Iskusstvo kino* 3 (1982): 84–99.

———. "Problema vzaimodeistviia iskusstv i neosushchestvelnnyi mul'tfil'm Fernana Lezhe 'Charli-kubist.'" In *Problemy sinteza v khudozhestvennoi kul'ture*, edited by Anatolii Prokhorov, Boris Raushenbakh, and Fëdor Khitruk, 76–99. Moscow: Nauka, 1985.

———. "'Organicheskaia mashina' u Eisenshteina i Disneia." *Kinovedcheskie zapiski* 34 (1997): 52–59.

Ivanov-Vano, Ivan. *Kadr za kadrom.* Moscow: Iskusstvo, 1980.

Ivanov-Vano, Ivan, and Anatolyi Volkov. *Khudozhniki sovetskogo mul'tfil'ma.* Moscow: Sovetskii Khudozhnik, 1978.

Izvolova, Irina. "Drugoe prostranstvo." In *Kinematograph ottepeli*, edited by Vitalii Troianovskii, 1: 77–99. Moscow: Materik, 1996.

Jakobson, Roman. "The Dominant." In *Readings in Russian Poetics. Formalist and Structuralist Views*, edited by Ladislav Matejka and Krystyna Pomorska, 82–87. Ann Arbor: Michigan Slavic Publications, 1978.

Kapkov, Sergei. "Golosa animatsii." In *Katalog-al'manakh. Otkrytii rossiskii festival' animatsionnogo kino*, edited by Sergei Serëgin, 106–111. Berezovaia Roshcha: Tretii otkrytii festival' animatsionnogo kino, 1998.

———, ed. *Entsiklopediia otechestvennoi mul'tiplikatsii.* Moscow: Algoritm, 2006.

———. "Viktor Smirnov: ot Disneia k 'Soiuzmul'tfil'mu' i dalee - v zabvenie..." Kino-teatr.ru, August 4, 2019. https://www.kino-teatr.ru/kino/art/kino/5417/.

Kelly, Catriona. *Refining Russia: Advice Literature, Polite Culture, and Gender from Catherine to Yeltsin.* Oxford: Oxford University Press, 2001.

———. "Riding the Magic Carpet: Children and Leader Cult in the Stalin Era." *The Slavic and East European Journal* 49, no. 2 Special Forum Issue: Russian Children's Literature: Changing Paradigms (Summer 2005): 199–224.

Khalatov, N. "Kogda otkazyvaiutsia ot zhanra." *Iskusstvo kino* 3 (1957a): 114–116.

———. "Rasti, Murzilka!" *Iskusstvo kino* 4 (1957b): 106–107.

Khaniutin, A. "Mul'tiplikatsiia i zritel'." *Iskusstvo kino* 8 (1981): 85–99.

Khitruk, Fëdor. "Kanikuly Bonifatsiia." Knizhnaia polka, n.d. http://books.rusf.ru/unzip/add-on/xussr_ty/hitruf11.htm?1/2.

———. "Toptyzhka." Knizhnaia polka, n.d. http://books.rusf.ru/unzip/add-on/xussr_ty/hitruf12.htm?1/1.

———. "Moi 'Soiuzmul'tfil'm.'" *Iskusstvo kino* 6 (1996a): 36–39.

———. "Sto vosem' vstrech." *Iskusstvo kino* 12 (1966b): 49–54.

———. "Vsegda v puti." *Iskusstvo kino* 4 (1966c): 117–121.

———. "Proverit' praktikoi!" *Iskusstvo kino* 7 (1968): 55–56.

———. "Kanikuly Bonifatsiia. Po motivam cheshkogo pisatelia Milana Matsoureka 'Bonifatsii i ego rodstvenniki.'" In *Fil'my skazki. Stsenarii risovannykh fil'mov. Vypusk 10*, edited by Iu. Belousov, 163–181. 10. Moscow: Iskusstvo, 1972.

———. "The Future Is Our Responsibility." *Soviet Film* 10 (1973): 30–32.

———. "Uchitel' i agitator." *Iskusstvo kino* 2 (1976): 68–70.

———. "Iskatel'." *Iskusstvo kino* 4 (1980): 128–129.

———. "From Thought to Image." *Soviet Film* 8 (1981): 27–28.

———. "V.P. Stepantsev." *Iskusstvo kino* 10 (1983): 135–136.

———. "Mul'tiplikatsiia v kontekste khudozhestvennoi kul'tury." In *Problemy sinteza v khudozhestvennoi kul'ture*, edited by Boris Raushenbakh, Anatolii Prokhorov, and Fëdor Khitruk, 7–24. Moscow: Nauka, 1985a.

———. "Pridumav mir, v nego poverit'." *Iskusstvo kino* 9 (1985b): 51–61.

————. "Poniat' dazhe to, chto trudno voobrazit'." *Iskusstvo kino* 6 (1986): 18–26.

————. *Russko-angliiskii slovar' animatsionnyx terminov.* Moscow: Vysshie kursy stsenaristov i rezhisserov, Pespekt, 1991.

————. "Sled v dushe." In *Kogda luna vmeste s solntsem*, edited by Aelita Romanenko, 178–187. TID Kontinent-Press, 2002.

————. "Metodicheskie ukazaniia k uchebnoi programme po distsipline 'Tekhnika odushevleniia.'" *Kinovedcheskie zapiski* 73 (2005a): 129–133.

————. "Mysli velikie, sredine i pesika Pafika." *Kinovedcheskie zapiski* 73 (2005b): 66–89.

————. "O fil'makh. O zarozhdenii idei fil'ma." *Kinovedcheskie zapiski* 73 (2005c): 50–65.

————. "Professiia - animator." *Kinovedcheskie zapiski* 73 (2005d): 39–49.

————. "Rasskazy ob animatorakh." *Kinovedcheskie zapiski* 73 (2005e): 204–211.

————. "'Situatsiia u vas dostatochno obeshchaiushchaia.' (Stenogramma zaniatiia v masterskoi F. Khitruka na Vysshikh kursakh stsenaristov i rezhisserov 14 ianvaria 1987)." *Kinovedcheskie zapiski* 73 (2005f): 123–126.

————. "Stsenarii mul'tfil'ma (konspekt lektsii)." *Kinovedcheskie zapiski* 73 (2005g): 134–136.

————. "Uchebnaia programma podgotovki rezhisserov-animatorov." *Kinovedcheskie zapiski* 73 (2005h): 126–128.

————. "Vospominaniia." *Kinovedcheskie zapiski* 73 (2005i): 8–38.

————. "Zhal', chto k chudu privykaiut." *Kinovedcheskie zapiski* 73 (2005j): 7.

————. "Energiia poiska." In *Professiia-animator*, edited by Fëdor Khitruk, 1: 298–302. Moscow: Gaiatri, 2007a.

————. *Professiia-animator.* Vol. 1. 2 vols. Moskva: Gaiatri, 2007b.

————. *Professiia-animator.* Vol. 2. 2 vols. Moskva: Gaiatri, 2007c.

————. "Pravila zhizn'." *Esquire*, March 19, 2010. https://esquire.ru/rules/286-fedor-hitruk/#part1.

————. "Khitruk o Khitruke." In *Vek Fëdora Khitruka. Katalog vystavki*, edited by Pavel Shvedov and Natalia Avdeeva, 12–15. St. Petersburg: Galereia iskusstv KGallery, 2017.

————. "Prodaetsia zemlia. Stsenarii animatsionnogo fil'ma." *Iskusstvo kino* 7/8 (2022): 150–157.

Khitruk, Fëdor, and Sergei Asenin. "Kuda idet mul'tiplikatsiia." *Iskusstvo kino* 9 (1977): 59–69.

Khitruk, Fëdor, and Aleksei Khaniutin. "Samoe 'detskoe' iskusstvo." *Iskusstvo kino* 7 (1982): 37–52.

Khitruk, Fëdor, and Natalia Lukinykh. "Stepen' neveroiatnosti." *Iskusstvo kino* 4 (1993): 122–129.

Khitruk, Fëdor et al. "Govoriat mastera ekrana." *Sovetskoe kino* 42 (1965).

Khitruk, Fëdor et al. "Svoboda vybora." *Iskusstvo kino* 2 (1990): 17–19.

Khrzhanovskii, Andrei. "Fëdor Khitruk." In *Rezhissery i khudozhniki sovetskogo mul'tiplikatsionnogo kino*, edited by Nataliia Venzher, 57–64. Moscow: Soiuzinformkino, 1984a.

————. "Fyodor Khitruk." *Soviet Film* 6 (1984b): 36–38.

————. "A Most Amusing Talent." *Soviet Film* 5 (1985): 28–30.

————. "Byvaiut strannye sblizheniia..." *Kinovedcheskie zapiski* 42 (1999): 165–173.

Khrzhanovskii, Andrei, and Fëdor Khitruk. "Fëdor Khitruk - Andrei Khrzhanovskii. Besedy pri iasnoi lune." *Kinovedcheskie zapiski* 52 (2001): 59–97.

Klado, N. "Tarakanishche." *Iskusstvo kino* 4 (1964): 45–47.

Kleiman, Naum. "K publikatsii issledovaniia Sergeia Èizenshteina ob Uolte Disnee." In *Problemy sinteza v khudozhestvennoi kul'ture*, edited by Anatolii Prokhorov, Boris Raushenbakh, and Fëdor Khitruk, 205–208. Moscow: Nauka, 1985.

Kononenko, Natalie. "The Politics of Innocence: Soviet and Post-Soviet Animation on Folklore Topics." *Journal of American Folklore* 124, no. 494 (2011): 272–294.

Konstantinovich, Valerii. *Esteticheskaia priroda mul'tiplikatsionnogo fil'ma*. Moscow: Akademiia obshchestvennykh nauk, 1990.

Konstantinovskii, Mailen. *Koapp! Koapp! Koapp!* 8 vols. Moscow: Iskusstvo, 1970.

Kostyukevich, Mariia. "Rossiiskaia animatsiia v shkatulke s sekretom." *Sk-Novosti*, April 18, 2016.

Kracauer, Siegfried. *Theory of Film. The Redemption of Physical Reality*. Princeton, NJ: Princeton University Press, 1960.

Kriukova, Antonina. "Khitruk - nasha vselennaia." *Animalife* (blog), May 13, 2012. http://animalife.ru/2012/05/13/xitruk-nasha-vselennaya/.

Krivulia, Natal'ia. "Osnovnye tendentsii avtorskikh animatsii Rossii 60–90kh godov." VGIK, 2001.

———. *Labirinty animatsii. Issledovanie khudozhestvennogo obraza rossiiskikh animatsionnykh fil'mov vtoroi poloviny XX veka*. Moscow: Izdatel'skii dom Graal', 2002.

Kurchevskii, Vadim. *Izobrazitel'noe reshenie mul'tiplikatsionnogo fil'ma. O prirode groteska i metafory*. Moscow: VGIK, 1986.

———. "'Rabotat' s Khitrukom trudno...'." In *Professiia animator*, edited by Fëdor Khitruk, 2: 280–281. Moscow: Gaiatri, 2007.

———. *Kliuchi k ekrannomu tvorchestvu. Rasskazy o mul'tiplikatsii*. Moscow: Moscovskii detskii fond, 2014.

Kushnirov, M. "Boevoi Kinosbornik No...." *Iskusstvo Kino* 2 (1967): 15–17.

Lagina, Natal'ia. "Mul'tipliktsiia: Lirika i Epos." *Iskusstvo Kino* 11 (1971): 82–87.

Leiborn, Kit. "Animatsionnaia kniga. (Perevod F. Khitruka)." Translated by Fëdor Khitruk. *Kinovedcheskie zapiski* 73 (2005): 137–203.

Leslie, Esther. *Hollywood Flatlands. Animation, Critical Theory and the Avant-Garde*. London, New York: Verso, 2002.

Lotman, Iurii. "The Semiosphere." In *Universe of the Mind: A Semiotic Theory of Culture*, translated by Ann Shukman, 123–214. London, New York: I.B. Tauris & Co. Ltd., 1990a.

———. *Universe of the Mind : A Semiotic Theory of Culture*. London, New York: I.B. Tauris, 1990b.

———. "Fenomen kul'tury." In *Izbrannye stat'i v trekh tomakh*, 1: 34–45. Tallin: Aleksandra, 1992.

———. *Ob iskusstve*. Sankt-Peterburg: Iskusstvo-SPB, 1998.

———. "Vnutri mysliashchikh mirov." In *Semiosfera*, 150–390. Sankt Peterburg: Iskusstvo-SPB, 2001.

MacFadyen, David. Yellow Crocodiles and Blue Oranges: Russian Animated Film Since World War Two. Montreal: McGill-Queen's University Press, 2005.

Macheret, Aleksandr, and Nina Glagoleva, eds. *Sovetskie khudozhestvennye fil'my. 1961–1979. Annotirovannyi katalog. Gosfil'mofond SSSR.* Vol. 5. Moscow: Iskusstvo, 1979.

Maisetti, Massimo. *I maestri di Mosca. Il cinema d'animazione russo dagli inizi ad oggi.* Milano: ISCA, 1988.

———. "Il cinema di animazione sovietico." *Letture* 458 (1989): 487–506.

Maliukova, Larisa. "Kuda idem my s piatachkom." *Iskusstvo kino* 6 (1996): 29–35.

———. "Disney - kak nashe vse." In *Katalog - al'manakh. Suzdal' 2002*, edited by Sergei Serëgin, 91–94. Suzdal': Otkrytyi rossiskogo festivalia animatsionnogo kino, 2002a.

———. "Poteriav, ne chuvstvoval sebia poteriannym." *Novaia Gazeta* 31 (April 29, 2002b). https://content.novayagazeta.ru/posts/2002/04/29/15094-poteryav-ne-chuvstvoval-sebya-poteryannym?amp=true.

———. "Fëdor Savel'yevich, kak nam budet ne khvatat' Vas!," Novaia Gazeta December 3, 2012a. https://novayagazeta.ru/articles/2012/12/03/52623-fedor-savelievich-kak-nam-budet-ne-hvatat-vas.

———. "Nu vot, poproshchalis' s Fëdorom Savel'evichem." *Novaia Gazeta*, December 5, 2012b. https://novayagazeta.ru/articles/2012/12/05/52653-nu-vot-poproschalis-s-fedorom-savelievichem.

———. *Sverkh Kino. Sovremennaia rossiiskaia animatsiia. Seriia Biblioteka Assotsiatsii Animatsionnogo kino,* St. Petersburg: Umnaia Masha, 2013.

———. "Fil'm kak bolevoi refleks." In *Vek Fëdora Khitruka. Katalog vystavki*, edited by Pavel Shvedov and Natalia Avdeeva, 22–27. St. Petersburg: Galereia iskusstv KGallery, 2017.

Maltin, Leonard. *Of Mice and Magic. A History of American Animated Cartoons.* Revised. New York: Plume, 1987.

———. *O myshakh i magii. Istoriia amerikanskogo risovannogo fil'ma.* Translated by Fëdor Khitruk. Moscow: Izdatel'stvo Dedinskogo, 2018.

Margolina, Irina. "'Pridia iz neizvestnosti, ia i ukhozhu, v neizvestnost'...' Nikolai Khodataev o prichinakh svoego ukhoda iz mul'tiplikatsii." *Kinovedcheskie zapiski* 52 (2001): 186–190.

Margolina, Irina, and Natal'ia Lozinskaia, eds. *Nashi Mul'tfil'my.* Moscow: Interros, 2006.

Marx, Karl. *The Capital (Das Kapital).* 3 vols. Hamburg: Verlag von Otto Meisner, 1867.

Marx, Karl, and Friedrich Engels. *Manifest der Kommunistischen Partei.* Veröffentlicht im Februar 1848. London: Gedruckt in der Office der "Bildungs-Gesellshaft für Arbeiter" von J. E. Burghard, February 1848.

Meyerhold, Vsevolod. "Chaplin i chaplinizm." In *Puti k sintezu. Meyerhol'd i kino*, edited by Aleksandr Fevral'skii, 212–234. Moscow: Iskusstvo, 1978.

Migunov, Evgenii. "S tochki zreniia zhivogo pokoinika." In *Katalog-al'manakh. Tarusa 99*, edited by Sergei Serëgin, 109–112. Berezovaia Roshcha: Chetvertyi otkrytii rossiiskii animatsionnogo kino, 1999.

———. "O Khitruke." In *Katalog-al'manakh. Suzdal' 2002*, edited by Sergei Serëgin, 113–120. Suzdal': Otkrytyi rossiiskii festival' animatsionnogo kino, 2002.

———. "Ob uslovnosti (Fragment iz esse 'Gde zhivet Baba-Iaga?')." In *Katalog-al'manakh. Suzdal' 2003*, edited by Sergei Serëgin, 120–135. Suzdal': VIII Otkrytyi rossiiskii festival' animatsionnogo kino, 2003.

Mikhailin, Iurii. "Vysshie formy – 'Za den' do nashei ery' Fëdora Khitruka i Iuriia Norsteina." *Seance*, May 1, 2020. https://seance.ru/articles/khitruk-norshtein-day-before/.

———. "'Liubimyi uchitel'-drug' – pamiati Vladimira Zuikova." *Seance*, March 3, 2021. https://seance.ru/articles/vladimir-zuykov-in-memoriam/.

Milne, Alan Alexander. *Vinni-Pukh i vse ostal'nye*. Translated by Boris Zakhoder. Moscow: Detskii Mir, 1960.

Milne, Alan Alexander, and Ernest H. Shepard. *Winnie-the-Pooh*. New York: E. P. Dutton and Co., 1926.

Mjolsness, Lora Wheeler. "Under the Hypnosis of Disney: Ivan Ivanov-Vano and Soviet Animation for Children." In *A Companion to Soviet Children's Literature and Film*, 2020, 389–416.

Mogl, Verena. *Juden, die ins Lied sich retten - der Komponist Mieczyslaw Weinberg (1919–1996) in der Sowjetunion*. Münster: Waxmann, 2019.

Morreall, John, ed. *The Philosophy of Laughter and Humor*. Albany: SUNY Press, 1987.

Mukařovský, Jan. *Structure, Sign, and Function: Selected Essays*. Yale Russian and East European Studies 14. New Haven, CT: Yale University Press, 1977.

"Mul'tiplikatsiia segodnia." *Iskusstvo kino* 9 (1967): 65–71.

Munitich, P. "Sovremennost' iskusstva mul'tiplikatsii. Nastoiashchee i budushchee rasvivaiushchegosia iskusstva." *Novosti ASIFA* 1 (1977).

Music-Weinberg. "Mieczysław Weinberg. The Composer and His Music," n.d. http://www.music-weinberg.net/index.html.

Nazarov, Eduard. "Neskol'ko slov ko dniu rozhdeniia. F. S. Khitruku 70 let." *Sovetskii Ekran* 12 (1987): 12–13.

———. "Dom na Kaliaevskoi." *Iskusstvo kino* 6 (1996): 40–43.

———. "Edik! Est' neplokhaia ideia..." In *Professiia-animator*, edited by Fëdor Khitruk, 282–286. Moscow: Gaiatri, 2007.

Nikitkina, Elena. "Sotsial'no-nravstvennaia problematika i novyi geroi v sovetskoi mul'tiplikatsii 70–80-x godov." In *Sovetskii mnogonatsional'nyi kinematograf na sovremennom etape*, edited by Marat Vlasov, 61–72. Sbornik nauchnykh trudov. Moskva: VGIK, 1983.

Norstein, Iurii. "Priznanie masteru." *Iskusstvo kino* 8 (1987): 74–78.

———. "Lektsii dlia slushatelei Vysshikh stsenarnykh i rezhisserskikh kursov Goskino SSSR. Lektsia 1." In *Animatograficheskie zapiski*, edited by Anatolii Prokhorov, 1: 18–31. Moskva: Animatograficheskii tsentr "Pilot," 1991a.

———. "Vse eto bylo by smeshno..." *Iskusstvo kino* 10 (1991b): 136–147.

———. "Prostranstvo skazki." *Iskusstvo kino* 3 (1997): 70–83.

———. "On vnes inoe ponimanie izobrazheniia..." *Kinovedcheskie zapiski* 73 (2005): 90–102.

———. "On vnes inoe ponimanie izobrazheniia..." In *Professiia-animator*, edited by Fëdor Khitruk, 231–248. Moscow: Gaiatri, 2007a.

———. "Priznanie masteru." In *Professiia-animator*, edited by Khitruk, 297–303. Moscow: Gaiatri, 2007b.

———. *Sneg na trave*. 2 vols. Moscow: Krasnaia Ploshchad', 2008.

———. "Chuvstvo balansa." In *Vek Fëdora Khitruka. Katalog vystavki*, edited by Pavel Shvedov and Natalia Avdeeva, 16–21. St. Petersburg: Galereia iskusstv KGallery, 2017.

———. "Iurii Norstein o rabote nad fil'mom 'Za den' do nashei ery.'" *Seance*, May 18, 2020. https://seance.ru/articles/norshtein-day-before/.

Ol'shvang, O., ed. *Vinni-Pukh i vse-vse-vse...Eduard Nazarov. Vladimir Zuikov. Materialy k vystavke khudozhnikov.* Moscow: Galereia na solianke, 2005.

Orlov, Aleksei. "Dvizhenie stilia." *Iskusstvo kino* 11 (1986): 72–82.

————. "Tra Disney e Zagabria. Le peculiarità stilistiche nell'animazione dell' Est-Europa." In *Animania. 100 anni di esperimenti nel cinema d'animazione*, 55–62. Milano: Bruno di Marino, 1998.

Pervyi Kanal. "Iubiliei otmechaet legendarnii khudozhnik-mul'tiplikator Fëdor Khitruk." *Novosti.* May 1, 2012. https://www.1tv.ru/news/2012-05-01/91120-yubiley_otmechaet_legendarnyy_hudozhnik_multiplikator_fedor_hitruk.

Petrov, Aleksandr, and Mikhail Tumelia. "Nauka udivliat'." *Kinovedcheskie zapiski* 73 (2005): 103–122.

Pikkov, Ülo. "On the Topics and Style of Soviet Animated Films." *Baltic Screen Media Review* 4 (2016): 17–37.

Pintus, Mario. "*I maghi dell'Est. Fantastico viaggio nel disegno animato dell'Europa orientale.*" Sassari: A.S. Sassu, 1987.

Pirandello, Luigi. *L'umorismo.* Second edition. Firenze: Luigi Battistelli, 1920. https://www.gutenberg.org/cache/epub/56958/pg56958-images.html#cap2-1.

Piretto, Gianpiero. *Quando c'era l'URSS. 70 anni di storia culturale sovietica.* Milano: Raffaello Cortina Editore, 2020.

Politicheskaia tema v mul'tiplikatsionnom kino. (Stenogramma dvustoronnego simpoziuma mul'tiplikatorov SSSR i GDR). Moskva: Soiuz kinematografistov SSSR, 1973.

Pontieri, Laura. Personal Interview with Fëdor Khitruk, October 12, 2005.

————. "Russian Animated Films of the 1960s as a Reflection of the Thaw: Ambiguities and Violation of Boundaries in Story of a Crime." *Studies in Russian and Soviet Cinema* 3, no. 1 (2009): 53–70.

————. Phone Interview with Sergei Alimov, January 31, 2012a.

————. *Soviet Animation and the Thaw of the 1960s. Not Only for Children.* New Barnet: John Libbey Publishing, 2012b.

Poš, Jan. *Výtarníci animovaného filmu.* Praha: Odeon, 1990.

Prokhorov, Alexander. "Winnie-the-Pooh. Vinni Pukh." In *Directory of World Cinema. Russia 2*, edited by Birgit Beumers, 300–302. Bristol; Chicago, IL: Intellect, 2015.

Prokhorov, Anatolii. "Èvolutsiia animatografa: ot mul'tiplikatsii k 'fantomu svobody.'" In *Mul'tiplikatsiia, animatograf, fantomatika...*, 31–59. Kiev: Izdaniie Pervogo Vsesoiuznogo Festivalia mul'tiplikatsionnykh fil'mov 'Krok-89", 1989.

————. "K filosofii animatsii." *Kinovedcheskie zapiski* 10 (1991a): 126–136.

————. "Vvedenie. Animatograf v kontekste ekrannoi kul'tury." In *Animatograficheskie zapiski*, edited by Anatolii Prokhorov, 1: 5–17. Moskva: Animatograficheskii tsentr "Pilot," 1991b.

————, ed. Animatograficheskie zapiski. Vypusk 1. Moscow: Animatograficheskii tsentr "Pilot", Nauchno-issledovatel'skii institut kul'tury, 1991.

Reid, Susan E. "The Khrushchev Kitchen: Domesticating the Scientific-Technological Revolution." *Journal of Contemporary History* 40, no. 2, Domestic Dreamworlds: Notions of Home in Post-1945 Europe (April 2005): 289–316.

Rimsky-Korsakov, Nikolai. *The Legend of the Invisible City of Kitezh (Skazanie o nevidimom grade Kitezhe i deve Fevronni) 1903–1904.* n.d. Opera, 4 acts.

Rudenko, Evgenii. "Zhil-byl mul't: Eduard Nazarov - ob upadke kul'tury i iade Gollivuda. Interview with Eduard Nazarov." *Argumenty i fakty*, March 17, 2012. https://aif.ua/culture/cinema/964049.

"Satiricheskii kinozhurnal 'Diatel'." *Iskusstvo kino* 9 (1959): 98.

Serebrovskii, Vladimir. "Sergei Alimov." In *Sovetskiie khudozhniki teatra i kino 77/78*, edited by Vera Kuleshova, 76–84. Moscow: Sovetskii khudozhnik, 1980.

Shatunovsky, I. "Sto shagov 'Fitilia.'" *Iskusstvo Kino* 12 (1970): 71–80.

Shklovsky, Viktor. *Za sorok let. Stat'i o kino*. Moscow: Iskusstvo, 1965.

———. *Theory of Prose*. Third printing. Russian Literature Series. Normal, IL: Dalkey Archive Press, 1998.

Shvedov, Pavel. "Kto sozdal 'Toptyzhku' i 'Kanikuly Bonifatsiia'?" Animalife (blog), January 17, 2013. http://animalife.ru/2013/01/17/kto-sozdal-toptyzhku-i-kanikuly-bonifaciya/.

———. "Bratstvo Khitruka." In *Vek Fëdora Khitruka. Katalog vystavki*, edited by Pavel Shvedov and Natalia Avdeeva, 10–11. St. Petersburg: Galereia iskusstv KGallery, 2017.

Shvedov, Pavel, and Natalia Avdeeva, eds. *Vek Fëdora Khitruka. Katalog vystavki*. St. Petersburg: Galereia iskusstv KGallery, 2017.

Shvedov, Pavel, Boris Pavlov, Mikhail Aldashin, and Aleksandr Uskov. *Fëdor Khitruk. Bonifatsii, Vinni-Pukh, Fil'm, Fil'm, Fil'm... Katalog vystavki*. Moscow: Galereia na solianke, 2009.

Silant'eva, T. "Sed'moe iskusstvo." *Tvorchestvo* 9 (1967): 15–17.

Silina, Maria. "The Struggle Against Naturalism. Soviet Art from the 1920s and 1950s." *Canadian Art Review* 41, no. 2. The Nature of Naturalism: A Trans-Historical Examination (2016): 91–104.

"Smelee iskat' novoe v mul'tiplikatsionnom kino!" *Iskusstvo kino* 2 (1959): 93–100.

Smoliarova, Nataliia. "Detskii 'nedetskii' Vinni-Pukh." In *Veselye chelovechki: kul'turnye geroi sovetskogo detstva. Sbornik statei*, edited by Il'ya Kukulin, Mark Lipovetskii, Mariia Maiofis, 287–314. Moscow: Novoe literaturnoe obozrenie, 2008.

"Soiuzmul'tfil'm otchityvaetsia." *Iskusstvo kino* 3 (1966): 52.

Stanislavsky, Constantin. *Creating a Role*, edited by Hermine Popper. Translated by Elizabeth Reynolds Hapgood. London: Bloomsbury, 2013.

Syrkina, Flora. "Rol' khudozhnika v izobrazitel'nom reshenii mul'tfil'ma." In *Sovetskiie khudozhniki teatra i kino*, edited by Vera Kuleshova, 7: 170–185. Moskva: Sovetskii khudozhnik, 1986.

Tereshchenko, Masha. "Opustevshii ostrov." kino-teatr.ru, December 3, 2012a. https://www.kino-teatr.ru/blog/y2012/12-3/319/.

———. "Rossiia mezhdu dvumia 'Vinni-Pukhami.'" Kino-teatr.ru, July 10, 2012b. https://www.kino-teatr.ru/blog/y2012/7-10/270/.

Troianovskii, Vitalii. "Chelovek Ottepeli (50-e Gody)." In *Kinematograph Ottepeli*, edited by Vitalii Troianovskii, 1: 5–77. Moscow: Materik, 1996.

Tsivian, Yuri. *Ivan the Terrible*. London: British Film Institute, 2002.

———. "Charlie Chaplin and His Shadows: On Laws of Fortuity in Art." *Critical Inquiry* 40, no. 3 (2014): 71–84.

Tsizin, I. "Fil'my-Skazki." *Iskusstvo Kino* 11 (1959): 137–138.

Tumelia, Mikhail. *Fazovka. Vse, chto vy khoteli znat' o fazovke no stesnialis' sprosit'...* Moscow: Moskovskaia animatsionnaia studiia Pilot. Proekt MLO, 1998.

Tumelia, Mikhail, and Aleksandr Petrov. "Nauka udivliat'." In *Professiia-animator*, edited by Fëdor Khitruk, 248–275. Moscow: Gaiatri, 2007.

Tynianov, Iurii. "Podporuchik Kizhe." In *Sochineniia: v trekh tomakh*, with introduction and commentary by B. Kostelianets, 1: 325-356. Leningrad: Gos. izd. khudozhnoi literatury, 1959.

Uayteker, Garol'd, and Dzhon Khalas. *Taiming v animatsii*. Translated by Fëdor Khitruk. Moscow: Magazin iskusstva, 2001.

"U nas v gostiakh." *Iskusstvo kino* 10 (1962): 69–80.

"Umer Fëdor Khitruk," *Gazeta*. December 3, 2012. https://www.gazeta.ru/culture/2012/12/03/a_4877245.shtml.

Vartanov, Anri. "Sekret uspekha." *Iskusstvo kino* 12 (1975): 72–80.

Vasil'kova, Aleksandra. "Fëdor Khitruk." In *Nashi mul'tfil'my*, edited by Irina Margolina and Natal'ia Lozinskaia, 124–131. Moscow: Interros, 2006.

Venzher, Nataliia. *Sotvorenie fil'ma ili neskol'ko interv'iu po sluzhebnym voprosam.* Moskva: Kinotsentr, 1990.

———. "Mesto vstrechi - teleekran." In *Katalog-al'manakh. Tarusa 99*, 113–117. Berezovaia Roshcha: Chetvertyi otkrytii rossiiskii animatsionnogo kino, 1999.

Verrocchio, Andrea del. *Equestrian Statue of Bartolomeo Colleoni*. n.d. Bronze. 1480–1488, 395 cm. Venice.

Volkov, Anatolii. *Mul'tiplikatsionnyi fil'm*. Moscow: Znanie, 1974a.

———. "Plokho Robinzonu..." *Iskusstvo kino* 10 (1974b): 67–70.

———. "Novoe i privychnom." *Iskusstvo kino* 3 (1976a): 76–80.

———. "S"est li volk zaitsa? Razmyshleniia o probleme geroia seriinykh mul'tfil'mov." In *Ekran 74/75*, edited by Galina Dolmatovskaia and El Bauman, 130–135. Moskva: Iskusstvo, 1976b.

———. "Fëdor Khitruk. Razgovor o professii." In *Mudrost' vymysla. Mastera mul'tiplikatsii o sebe i svoem iskusstve*, edited by Sergei Asenin, 178–186. Moskva: Iskusstvo, 1983.

———. "Stilevye osobennosti sovremennogo mul'tiplikatsionnogo fil'ma." In *O khudozhnikakh teatra, kino i TV*, edited by V. V. Vanslov, 163–172. Leningrad: Khudozhnik RSFSR, 1984.

———. "Mul'tiplikatsiia." In *Kino. Politika i Liudi: 30-e Gody*, edited by L. Kh. Mamatova, 110–122. Moskva: Materik, 1995.

Voronina, Olga, ed. *A Companion to Soviet Children's Literature and Film.* Leiden: Brill, 2020.

Voronov, Boris, Evgenii Migunov, and Anatolii Sazonov. *Fil'my skazki: stsenarii risovannykh fil'mov*. Moskva: Goskinoizdat, 1950.

Wells, Paul. *Understanding Animation*. London, New York: Routledge, 1998.

———. *Animation: Genre and Authorship*. London, New York: Wallflower, 2002.

Whitaker, Harold, and John Halas. *Timing for Animation*. New York: Focal Press, 1981.

Yampolsky, Mikhail. "The Space of Animated Film. Khrzhanovsky's 'I Am with You Again' and Norstein's 'The Tale of Tales.'" *Afterimage* 13, Special Issue Animating The Fantastic. (1987): 93–117.

Zabolotskikh, D. "Skazka o sovershennom vremeni." *Iskusstvo kino* 10 (1998): 82–86.

Zagorodnikova, Anna. "Kollegi mul'tiplikatora Khitruka gotoviat pozdravleniia k ego 95-letiiu." *Ria Novosti*, May 1, 2012. https://ria.ru/20120501/638732542.html.

Zaitseva, Lidiia. *Evoliutsiia obraznoi sistemy sovetskogo fil'ma 60–80kh godov.* Moscow: VGIK, 1991.
Zakrzhevskaia, Liudviga. "Pritcha o cheloveke, kotoryi leleial ramku." In *Ekran.* *1966–1967*, edited by M. Dolinskii and S. Chertok, 53–55. Moscow: Iskusstvo, 1967a.
———. "Schastlivaia zakonomernost'." *Sovetskii Ekran* 2 (1967b). https://chapaev. media/articles/9162.
———. "Ot maski k obrazu." *Iskusstvo kino*, 1969, 6: 86–93.
———. "Na poroge velikoi zhizni." *Iskusstvo kino* 3 (1971): 78–84.
———. "Mul'tiplikatsiia zhdet dramaturga." *Iskusstvo kino* 7 (1973): 86–96.
Zlotnik, Olga. "Winnie-the-Pooh." *Soviet Film* 2 (1973): 37.
Zuikov, Vladimir. "Vse reshila sluchainost'." In *Professiia-animator*, edited by Fëdor Khitruk, 286–297. Moscow: Live Book, 2008.

Archival Material

"Delo Fil'ma 'Chelovek v Ramke,'" 1965. RGALI Soiuzmul'tfil'm fond 2469, opis' 4, ed. hkr.659.
"Delo Iunosha Fridrikh Engel's Soiuzmul'tfil'm," 1969. RGALI Soiuzmul'tfil'm fond 2469, opis' 4 ed. khr. 694.
"'Fil'm Fil'm Fil'm.' Literaturnyi Stsenarii F. S. Khitruka, V. A. Golovanova. Varianty," 1967. RGALI Soiuzmul'tfil'm fond 2469, opis' 4, ed. khr. 639.
"'Fil'm Fil'm Fil'm.' Rezhisserskii Stsenarii," 1967. RGALI Soiuzmul'tfil'm fond 2469, opis' 4, ed. khr.640.
"'Kanikuly Bonifatsiia' Stsenarii Mul'tiplikatsionnogo Fil'ma F. Khitruka (Po ska-zke cheshkogo pisatelia Milana Matsoureka 'Bonifatsii i ego rodstvenniki') -2 Chasti," 1964. RGALI Soiuzmul'tfil'm fond 2469, opis' 2, ed. khr. 120.
Khitruk, Fëdor. "'Za Den' Do Nashei Ery' - Stsenarnii Plan Mul'tiplikatsionnogo Fil'ma," November 15, 1976. RGALI Soiuzmul'tfil'm fond 2469, opis' 5, ed. khr. 183, p. 1–4. https://chapaev.media/articles/11363.
"Literaturnyi Stsenarii Fil'ma 'Chelovek v ramke.'" Moscow, 1965. RGALI Soiuzmul'tfil'm fond 2469, opis' 4, ed. khr.657.
"Stenogramma zasedanii khudozhestvennogo soveta studii po obsuzhdeniiu izgotovitel'novo perioda fil'mov: Rezhissera V. Polkovnikova 'Zelennyi zmii,' F. Khitruka 'Tishina.'" Moscow, 26/4 1962. RGALI Soiuzmul'tfil'm fond 2469, opis'1, ed. khr. 1207.
"Stenogramma zasedaniia khudozhdestvennogo soveta po obsuzhdeniiu literaturn-ogo stsenarii F. Khitruka, V. Golovanova 'Fil'm fil'm fil'm,'" March 21, 1967. RGALI Soiuzmul'tfil'm fond 2469, opis' 1, ed. khr. 42.
"Stenogramma zasedaniia khudozhdestvennogo soveta po obsuzhdeniiu rezhis-serskogo stsenariia F. Khitruka 'Fil'm Fil'm Fil'm,'" June 13, 1967. RGALI Soiuzmul'tfil'm fond 2469, opis' 4, ed. khr. 50.
"Stenogramma zasedaniia khudozhestvennogo soveta studii fil'ma rezhissera V. Dezhkina 'Chipollino,' rezhisserskikh stsenariev: Amal'rika 'Dve Skazki' i F. Khitruka 'Tishina.'" Moscow, 1962. RGALI Soiuzmul'tfil'm fond 2469, opis' 1, ed. khr. 1203.

"Toptyzhka. Mul'tiplikatsionnyi stsenarii Khitruka," June 1963. RGALI Soiuzmul'tfil'm fond 2469, opis' 2, ed. khr. 214.

"Toptyzhka. Protokol zasedeniia khudozhestvennogo soveta Ot 14.6.63," June 14, 1963. RGALI Soiuzmul'tfil'm fond 2469, opis' 2, ed. khr. 215.

"Zakliuchenie o literaturnom stsenarii risovannogo Fil'ma 'Fil'm Fil'm Fil'm,'" April 6, 1967. RGALI Soiuzmul'tfil'm fond 2469, opis' 4, ed. khr.641.

Appendix

Films Animated by Khitruk at Soyuzmultfilm

The Adventures of Buratino (Prikliucheniia Buratino). Directed by Dmitrii Babichenko, Ivan Ivanov-Vano, Mikhail Botov. 1959.

The Adventures of Mursilka. Part 1 (Prikliucheniia murzilki. Vyp. 1). Directed by Boris Stepantsev, Evgenii Raikovskii. 1956.

The Adventures of the Magic Globus or the Witches' Tricks (Prikliucheniia volshebnogo globusa ili prodelki ved'm). Directed by Ivan Aksenchuk. 1982.

Again a Bad Mark - Murzilka's Adventures. (Opiat' dvoika - Prikliucheniia Murzilki). Directed by Evgenii Raikovskii, Boris Stepantsev. 1957.

The Arrow Flies in the Tale (Strela uletaet v skazku). Directed by Leonid Amal'rik. 1954.

The Boy from Naples (Mal'chik iz Neapolia). Directed by I. Aksenchuk. 1958.

The Brave Hare (Khrabryi zaiats). Directed by Ivan Ivanov-Vano. 1955.

The Cat's House (Koshkin dom). Directed by Leonid Amal'rik. 1958.

Comrades-Friends (Druz'ia Tovarishchi). Directed by Viktor Gromov. 1951.

The Courageous Pak (Khrabryi Pak). Directed by E. Raikovskii, V. Degtiarev. 1953.

The Crow, The Fox, The Cuckoo and the Cock (Vorona i lisitsa, kukushka i petukh). Directed by Ivan Aksenchuk. 1953.

The Cuckoo and the Starling (Kukushka i skvorets). Directed by Vladimir Polkovnikov, Leonid Amal'rik. 1949.

A Dangerous Prank (Opasnaia shalost'). Directed by Evgenii Raikovskii. 1954.

Different wheels (Raznye kolesa). Directed by Leonid Amal'rik. 1960.

The Disobedient Kitten (Neposlushnyi kotenok). Directed by Mstislav Pashchenko. 1953.

The Dog and the Cat (Pes i kot). Directed by Lev Atamanov. 1955.

The Elephant and the Ant (Slon i muravei). Directed by Boris Dëzhkin. 1948.

Emergency Aid (Skoraia pomoshch'). Directed by Lamis Bredis. 1949.

The Enchanted Boy (Zakoldovannyi Mal'chik). Directed by Vladimir Polkovnikov, Aleksandra Snezhko-Blotskaia. 1955.

Exactly at 3:15 (Rovno v 3:15). Directed by Evgenii Migunov, Boris Dëzhkin. 1959.

An Extraordinary Match (Neobyknovennyi match). Directed by Boris Dëzhkin, Mstislav Pashchenko. 1955.

Familiar Pictures (Znakomye kartinki). Directed by Evgenii Migunov. 1957.

A Family Chronicle (Semeynaya khronika). Directed by Leonid Amal'rik. 1961.

Fedia zaitsev. Directed by Valentina Brumberg, Zinaida Brumberg. 1948.

Fly Tsokhotukha (Mukha-Tsokhotukha). Directed by Vladimir Suteev. 1941.

The Forest Adventurers (Lesnye puteshestvenniki). Directed by Mstislav Pashchenko. 1951.

The Fox-Builder (Lisa-stroitel'). Directed by Panteleimon Sazonov. 1950.

The Geese-Swans (Gusi-lebedy). Directed by Aleksandra Snezhko-Blotskaia, I. Ivanov, Lev Mil'chin, Nadezhda Stroganova. 1949.

The Girl in the Jungle (Devochka v dzhungliakh). Directed by Mikhail Tsekhanovskii. 1956.

The Goat Musician (Kozel-muzykant). Directed by Boris Dëzhkin. 1954.

Grandmother's Little Goat. A Tale for Adults (Babushkin kozlik. Skazka dlia vzroslykh). Directed by Leonid Amal'rik. 1963.

Great Troubles (Bol'shie nepriiatnosti). Directed by Valentina Brumberg, Zinaida Brumberg. 1961.

Hunter Fëdor (Okhotnik Fëdor). Directed by Aleksandr Ivanov. 1938.

I Drew the Little Man (Cheloveka narisoval ia). Directed by Valentina Brumberg, Zinaida Brumberg, Valentin Lalaiants. 1960.

In a Faraway Kingdom - By a Wave of the Wand (V nekotorom tsarstve - Po shchuch'emu veleniiu). Directed by Ivan Ivanov-Vano, Mikhail Botov. 1957.

Ivashko and Baba Yaga (Ivashko i Baba-Yaga). Directed by Valentina Brumberg, Zinaida Brumberg. 1938.

Kashtanka (Kashtanka). Directed by Mikhail Tsekhanovskii. 1952.

The Key (Kliuch). Directed by Lev Atamanov. 1961.

The Lion and the Hare (Lev i zaiats). Directed by Boris Dëzhkin, Gennadii Filippov. 1949.

A Little Liar (Lgunishka). Directed by Ivan Ivanov-Vano. 1938.

The Little Cub (Medvezhonok). Directed by Petr Nosov, Ol'ga Khodataeva, Aleksandr Evmenenko. 1940.

The Little Grey Neck (Seraia sheika). Directed by Leonid Amal'rik, Vladimir Polkovnikov. 1948.

The Little Red Flower (Alen'kii tsvetochek). Directed by Lev Atamanov. 1952.

The Magical Bell (Chudesnii kolokol'chik). Directed by Valentina Brumberg, Zinaida Brumberg. 1949.

The Magic Carpet (Volshebnyi kover). Directed by Lev Atamanov. 1948. Erevanskaia studiia.

The Magic Treasure (Volshebnyi klad). Directed by Dmitrii Babichenko. 1950.

The Magical Shop (Volshebnyi magazin). Directed by Leonid Amal'rik, Vladimir Polkovnikov. 1953.

Murzilka on the Sputnik (Murzilka na sputnike). Directed by Evgenii Raikovskii, Boris Stepantsev. 1960.

The Night Before Christmas (Noch' pered Rozhdestvom). Directed by Zinaida Brumberg, Valentina Brumberg. 1951.

Old Friends (Starye snakomye). Directed by Boris Dëzhkin, Mstislav Pashchenko. 1956.

On the Forest stage (Na lesnoi estrade). Directed by Ivan Aksenchuk. 1954.

An Orange Neck (Oranzhevoe gorlyshko). Directed by Vladimir Polkovnikov, Aleksandra Snezhko-Blotskaia. 1954.

Petia and Red Riding Hood (Petia i krasnaia shapochka). Directed by Boris Stepantsev, Evgenii Raikovskii. 1958.

The Princess Frog (Tsarevna-liagushka). Directed by Mikhail Tsekhanovskii. 1954.

Sarmiko. Directed by Ol'ga Khodataeva, Evgenii Raikovskii. 1952.

The Secret of the Far-Away Island (Taina dalekogo ostrova). Directed by Valentina Brumberg, Zinaida Brumberg. 1958.

The Seven-Color Flower (Tsvetik-semitsvetik). Directed by Mikhail Tsekhanovskii. 1948.

The Snow Postman. A New Year Tale (Snegovik-pochtovik. Novogodniaia skazka). Directed by Leonid Amal'rik. 1955.

The Snow Queen (Snezhnaia koroleva). Directed by Lev Atamanov. 1957.

The Sober Sparrow: A Tale for Adults. (Nep'iushchii vorobei. Skazka dlia vzroslykh). Directed by Leonid Amal'rik. 1960.

Soon There Will Be Rain (Skoro budet dozhd'). Directed by Vladimir Polkovnikov. 1959.

The Sporting Gun (Okhotnich'e ruzh'e). Directed by Panteleimon Sazonov, Roman Davydov. 1948.

Stëpa, the Sailor (Stëpa-Moriak). Directed by Valentina Brumberg, Zinaida Brumberg. 1955.

The Sturdy Fellow (Krepysh). Directed by Leonid Amal'rik, Vladimir Polkovnikov. 1950.

The Tale about the Dead Tsarevna and the Seven Bogatyrs (Skazka o mervoi tsarevne i semi bogatyriakh). Directed by Aleksandra Snezhko-Blotskaia, Ivan Ivanov-Vano. 1951.

The Tale of Chapaev (Skazka o Chapaeve). Directed by Mikhail Tsekhanovskii. 1958.

The Tale of the Fisherman and the Fish (Skazka o rybake i rybke). Directed by Mikhail Tsekhanovskii. 1950.

The Tale of the Good Umar (Skazka o dobrom Umar). Directed by Aleksandr Evmenenko. 1938.

The Tall Hill (Vysokaia gorka). Directed by Leonid Amal'rik, Vladimir Polkovnikov. 1951.

Trip to the Moon (Polet na lunu). Directed by Valentina Brumberg, Zinaida Brumberg. 1953.

The Twelve Months (Dvenadtsat' mesiatsev). Directed by Ivan Ivanov-Vano, Mikhail Botov. 1956.

Uncle Stëpa (Dyidya Stipa). Directed by Vladimir Suteev, Lamis Bredis. 1938.

Validub. Directed by Dmitrii Babichenko. 1952.

A Walnut Twig (Orekhovyi prutik). Directed by Ivan Aksenchuk. 1955.

What Kind of Bird is This? (Eto chto za ptitsa?). Directed by Evgenii Migunov. 1955.

When the Trees Light Up (Kogda zazhigaiutsia elki). Directed by Mstislav Pashchenko. 1950.

Index

Note: *Italic* page numbers refer to figures and page numbers followed by "n" denote endnotes.